# Chapter 1

You walk hurriedly.Half running,half walking.Your bag almost fell from your shoulder every 2 minutes because of your movement.You look at your watch,you sigh."Arghh!!",you almost scream as you scared of being late to school.You could see the school gate and you saw two prefect trying to close the gate.Thank god you almost near there.You just run a few steps and reached the gate.
"Sharon !!",you heard a rough man voice called your name.You slowly look behind the prefects and saw him.The guy who called you just now.You sigh.
"You're late......again..."he said while checking his small notebook that he took out from his pocket."This is the third time,from this week....and it's only been three days from the start of the week.Mind to tell me what happen??",he said and look at you in a fierce gaze.
"I'm sorry.I promise I won't be late again.",you said and look down."I hope I can trust you.Now go on.You'll be late for class",he said and set you off.You bow and walk away.
You reach inside the building and walk to the locker side.You reach your locker and as you're opening your locker,you could feel people staring at you.But,you're use to it.But still,you could feel a stare that could make hole in your head.You slowly turn around and saw her.You're ex-best friend,Minhwa.When she realise you were looking at her,she walk away and you could see a few girls follow her.
You turn back to your locker and grab a few books for the class.You closed back your locker door and walk away.

# Chapter 2

--------During recess-------
You pick up a tray and queue along with other students.You grab a few food.Everything looks good.Well,since you are in a private school,of course,even the food is expensive.You're father was the most respected bussinessman.But,because of a mistake you made two years ago,your family's name was humiliated.Eventhough the family's bussiness isn't damaged a lot,but still,your parents couldn't forgive you.Because people will remember your mistake forever.
You sat on the seat that you always had alone since no one come close to you since the mistake you made.You also always bullied by the students there.You used to had a best friend,but unfortunately,she left you too.So,you're standing alone,on your own in this world.But,you kept remind yourself that this is the last year of high school.You smile to yourself.
After 4 class,you finish your school.You pack your stuff and walk out of the school gate.You look at the ground as you were scared

to look at people in their face.You keep walking like that till
you reach your house.
You unlock your house and enter."Miss,do you want to eat
now?",your maid said.You shook your head and walk upstairs to
your room.
You put your bag on the ground and sat on your bed.You hug your
knees and tears collected in your eyes.
You have problems.But,the major problem is that you don't have
anybody to spill it all out.Not even your mother.
You lie down on your bed and cry yourself to sleep

Chapter 3

"Miss....miss",you felt a hand shake your body.You squint your
eyes open and saw a middle-aged woman in front of
you."Eo..girl",you sat up and rub your eyes.
"Your mother call you.For dinner",she said politely.You nod your
head."I'll be down in a minute.I'll change",you stand up and walk
to your closet.You wash up simply and wear pajama.
You tie your hair to a bun and walk downstairs.You saw your
parents talking.Then,your mother raise her head and look at
you."What took you so long?",she frown."Sorry.I was washing up
and.....",you try to explain.But she cut you."Just sit down.We
have something to tell you",she said while cutting her meat on
the plate.You nod and sat down on the chair accross her.
"We want to tell you something and we hope you would accept
it",your father said.You stare at your plate.Youe heart beats
fast."What is it about?The state is so tense",you thought to
yourself."What is it,appa?",you softly ask your father.
"You will get married to the son of a friend of mine.",he said it
loud and clear.That's it.You didn't know what to say.Yourind
didn't even work properly that time.You're still processing the
sentence.You look at your dad.Your eyes widened."What?",you
almost cry.
"I'm sorry.But this is the only way......","You don't have to
apologise.It's her fault.She has to be responsible now",your
mother cut your father."What do you mean?",you ask your
father."Don't be harsh on her.",your father said to your
mother."Harsh?Because of her,your company is almost bancrupt and
you said I'm harsh?",she frown at your father.Then,she look at
you."Because of you,your father had to contain shame.",she
burst.You just stare at her.
You stand up from the seat and walk to your room.You hug your
bear and cried."It's not my fault,omma.It really isn't.I didn't
do it",you whisper to yourself,hoping that she could hear you.You
were really depressed when your parents still blame you for the
mistake of 2 years ago.
After 2 hours,you were lying down on your bed.Dried tears on your
cheek,but you still sob.Then,you hear a knock on your door.

You turned to your door and saw your father."Mia,are you awake?",your father said softly."Dad",you call him softly.He walk to your bed and sat next to you.You hug him."Appa.It's not my fault.It's really not.I'm sorry if I embarassed you,but I don't want to get married.",you cried.

"I know,Sharon.I trust you.But,other people don't",your father said."Is it true,because of me,you almost bancrupt?",you ask him.He kept quiet."This is the only way to save my bussiness now.Its a new contract.But,you have to marry the son.",he said.You nod."Go to sleep.You have school tommorow.",you lie down and he cover you with your blanket.He kiss your forehead."When is the wedding?",you ask him."Next week",he said and walk

Chapter 4

He checking some of the documents on his table.He was so immersed in it even when his father enter,he didn't realise."Larry,can't you hear me?",his father called him a few times."Oh,dad.I'm sorry.I was reading those files",he stand up and bow to his father."It's okay.I need to talk to you about something",his father said and sat on the couch in his office. "Sure,what is it,dad?",he look at his father."You'll be marrying a girl that I chose for you.Next week.I know,you might be angry now.But,the contract with this company is huge.So,it'll be advantage for us",he said and smile."Which company?",Larry asked."Star Fire Company.Held by my friend",his father replied.He nod."But,getting married.Isn't that just a bit...",he doesn't know how to say it.

"You're a mature young man.I'm sure you could make it.I mean,she's not that bad",his father said."By the way,you ended your relationship last month.",he holds Larry's hand."I believe in you",he said and walk out.

As soon as his father walk out,he sat on his chair and text with his friends."Guys,meeting.NOW!",he send and walk out of his office.

Chapter 5

You wake up and wash up to go to school.You thought that you want to go to school early so that you don't have to meet your parents.Also,so that you won't be late to school again.

You walk slowly to school,with your head down,staring at the road you're walking."Getting married?Me?I'm too young",you thought to yourself.

You sat on the bench nearby the school gate,since nobody is at school yet.Your leg plays with a small rock."How could I be someone's wife at this age.I don't even know who this guy is",you said and closed your eyes.You sighed.You take out your smartphone and plays with it.You frown.Even when you play your game,you

still hears what your mother said last night.It didn't stop playing in your head.
You almost cry."Sharon ,nobody will believe you.Even if you tell them 1000 times,they will only believe what they want to believe.Go on wih your life",you whisper to yourself.
Students started to arrive at school.You walk inside and as usual,you walk to your locker.You really worried if school days becomes bad.But,thank god.Nothing happens.
-----------End of school-------
As you were walking to your house,your phone rang.You took it out from your pocket and look at the caller id.You smile."Dad!",you said loudly."Oh.Sharon,where are you now?",he ask."Still walking home from school",you reply."Ah.Once you're arrived home,get ready okay?I'll send my driver to pick you up at 5 pm.You're meeting him.",he said and ended your call."Him?",you were wondering what he meant until it hit you.Your eyes widened.You fastly walked home.
About 10 minutes walking,you arrived at your place and wash up and got ready.You don't know if you're excited or scared


Chapter 6

You put on a white floral dress.Then,you tie your hair into half braid.You also put on a thin makeup.Finish with the preparation,you walk downstairs and sat on the couch and wait for the driver.Your heart beats fast.Even you don't know if it beats fast because of excited or scared.You keep breathing in and out to control yourself."What if he's ugly?What if I'm not beautiful enough for him?What if he's a bad person?",you ask yourself.You frown and shake your head."Ah!I'm getting crazy!",you almost screamed.
After 1 hour of waiting,you hear a honk sound from outside."Ah!The car's arrived",you smile and put on your shoes.You walk out and greet the driver.He open the door for you and you step in the car.You sat in the car and the driver closed the door.You bit your lips.You don't know what to expect.
--------After some time---------
You arrived at a restaurant.A fancy restaurant.Your eyes widened as you never been to a fancy retaurant before eventhough you from a rich family.You step in the restaurant and saw a fancy chandelier up above you.Then,a guy stand in front of you."Yes?Do you have any reservation here?",he ask you."Williams family",you said and he check in the guest list."Williams Sharon?",he said again.You nod."Follow me please",he said and you follow him.
He open a door to a private eating room.You saw your father sitting with a middle-aged guy....then you saw him.You look at him and he was looking at you.Your first eye contact with him. "Ah,there she is.Sit here,next to me.",your father said.You walk and pull out the chair next to him.You sat in front of your husband-to-be."Meet my friend,Mr Brown.And his son,Lawrence",your father introduce the two person in front of you.You bow.

"Oh,his name is Lawrence",you thought to yourself."He's not that bad",you added."Good afternoon,I'm Sharon Williams ",you introduce yourself."Wah,she really pretty.Like her mother",Mr Brown said.You smiled.
----------While eating--------
"We thought of delaying your wedding",your dad said.Your eyes widened.You look at your dad."We thought that maybe you want to know each other first,so,we want to delay the wedding but,there's a catch",he said and smile."You guys will be living together,in a house that I bought",Mr Brown said.Your eyes turned to Mr Brown . "Dad",you called your father softly."So that you will be independant.Plus,you'll get to know each other better",he said to you.You frowned.You look down at your plate.You don't even know what to say,or to think.
----------Finish dinner--------
You step out of the restaurant with the other three guys."Well,goodnight.I'm looking forward for this wedding.At least our family have that bond",Mr Brown said.You just bow to him and step in your car.
While in the car,it was quiet.Then,your father start talking."What do you think of him?",he ask."He's not that bad",you replied."He's good at singing too",your father added.You nod."But dad,do we really have to live together?",you ask him."It's your mother idea.",he replied short."Of course",you whisper to yourself.


Chapter 7

"Start packing up.You'll be moving in with him tommorow",your mother said.You stare at the floor.She woke  you up from bed to tell you that."Finish school,come straight home.So,you'll have more time to pack",she added.You didn't move a muscle.
You walk to school with a little hope that you're day would be great.As usual,other students will look at you like you're some kind of an alien but you're used too it.It's been two years since the accident but nobody letting it go.
"Sharon!",you heard a scream in the class.You turned your head infront."Yes,teacher",you said and stood up from your chair."Meet me after class",she replied.You nod and sat down on your chair again.
~~~~~~~~~
"What's wrong,Sharon?Is something bothering you?",your teacher ask."I don't know if it's a problem or not",you said."What is it?Tell me",she said."I'm....I'm.....getting married",you said and look down on the floor.You felt ashamed."Oh,it's okay.You're not the only one who's getting married in this school.It's between bussiness?If that's the case then it's normal.",she said as she tried to calm you down."Yeah,but you know what the students call me,you know,after the accident that happens two years ago.Wonder what will they call me after they know about the

wedding",you said and cover your face with both of your palm."Don't worry.I'll keep it as a secret",she sure you.
---------Finish school-------
You waited for all the students to walk out of the school then you leave.You still not sure how to deal with other people staring at you.So,you always walks alone.

You walk to the school gate with your head down.You watch your feet stepping on the ground.But then,you feel the urge to raise your head.So,you did.

You saw a big black car in front of the gate.You wonder who it is.You never seen that car before.But,you just continue walking.Then,you saw the back door was open and.............he step out of the car.Your eyes widened.

You act like you don't know him but you walk faster."Sharon!",you heard him calls you.You stopped.You tilt your head to the left and saw the car next to you,with him in it.He slide the window down and you saw him looking at you.

You bit your lips.Your brain start thinking what you should do next.Then,you had an idea.You squat down to tie your shoe lace."Okay,hotshot.Let's see if you can catch me",you said.Finish tying your shoelace,you made a move like racing gesture."What are you doing?",he said from inside the car."1....2....3...GO!",you count and ran as fast as you can."Yah!",he scream.You laughed.It's been a while since you ran,even in sports event.Since the accident two years ago,you were not allowed to take part in anything that represent your school because they afraid that people would spread the bad news.

Reached your house you open the door and enter then close the door with your back.You laughed so hard.It's been a while since you laugh like this."What are you laughing at?",your mother said to you while going downstairs.You kept quiet."Where's Lawrence?",she add."How do you know that guy came to me?",you frown."I asked him to fetch you so that you would go straight to your new home.All of your stuffs are there",she said and fold her arms to her chest.

You ran upstairs to your bedroom to be sure what she said is true.And it is.All of your stuff is gone."I told you I semt all of your stuff to your new house.",she said as she lean at your door and fold her arms again."How could you do this to me?I'm not ready!!",you almost scream at her."Don't you dare raise your voice to me,young lady",she said.

Then,the doorbell rang."Go!He's here already.",she said and make way so that you would come out from your room.You slowly walk down with your head down."Good afternoon ,Mrs Williams",Lawrence greet your mom."Ah,yes.Please take care of my daughter.From now on,she's your responsibility",she said and laugh like nothing happen just now.

"Please follow me",Lawrence said.You nod and followed him to the car.Your head still looking down.He opened the door for you and you stepped in.

## Chapter 8

You open the door to the house and step in.You wait for Lawrence to enter to walk upstairs."Come.Let me show you your room",he said.You follow him.But your eyes wander around.The house is big.Then,you realise how rich your husband-to-be is."Doesn't mean I'll be happy with this big house",you thought to yourself. After follow him,he show you your room."Do you like the decorations?",he ask you.Your eyes widened.The room was so beautiful with pink and white curtains.Your bed is quite big too.You saw an Apple laptop on the study table."That's not mine",you said to him."Ah,I bought it.I thought that maybe you'll need it,for study",he said and walk away."Enjoy your room",he said.You smile."Maybe he's not bad at all",you said and jumped on your bed.You check on everything and yes,every stuff of yours is in the room.

[Larry's POV]

I lie down on my bed.I want to take some rest cause after this I have to do a lot of documents.She looks cute with her smile.Maybe this wedding is not that bad.I drifted to sleep after closing my eyes.

[Author POV]

--------At Night------

You took your bath and finished with it,you cover yourself with towel.A lot of things came to your mind.You're now living with a guy that you only know his name.Anything can happen.

You wear your white pajama and open your room door to go downstairs.You walk out and saw Chen walking on your way.You quickly looked down on the floor and lean against the wall.He stop walking right infront of you.He then turn his body to face you."You don't need to be scared of me",he said and continue walking to his office room.You look at his back as he walking and sigh.You're not ready for this.

You walked downstairs and look into the fridge.You grab a cold water bottle and drank it."Ah!",you thirst gone.You saw a bowl of congee on the table."Is this for me?",you said and took a smaller bowl and scoop some in the big bowl to your small bowl,in case he still haven't eaten."Wah!This is so delicious",you said to yourself and eat some more.

## chapter 9

"Come on.Get in the car.I'll send you to school",he said while putting on his shoes."No.I'll just walk.",you said and start walking out.

-------Reached School------

All the people look at you in a weird way.You know those gazes.It's the same gaze that they give you two years ago."What did I do this time?",you thought to yourself.Then,you saw your

ex-best friend,Minhwa look at you with a frown.You continue
walking to your locker.
"Hey.Look at the newspaper.Someone's getting married.Not just
that.The killer is getting married.How embarrasing",a girl scream
in the middle of the hallway.You raise your head as you hear what
the girl just said."Oh.Its true.Here.It's the front
page.Lizzy,isn't this your father's company's newspaper?",a boy
ask Lizzy,one of Maddi's friend.
"Yeah.Someone told me yesterday.",Lizzy replied.Your bag fell
from your grab.Your eyes widened."No way.Maybe....teacher?",you
thought to yourself."What's wrong,Sharon ?Ah!Isn't that
you?You're getting married,right?Why didn't you tell us?Why did
you tell teacher only?",Lizzy said again.You close your locker
and walk away.
You walk to the teacher's room and see your
teacher."Teacher!",you almost scream."What is it,Sharon?",she
ask."How could you?Why did you do it?",you ask her
again."Sharon,I don't understand what you're trying to say",she
replied.
You walk out of the room and walk out of school.Tears fell from
from your eyes.You ran home.You open the door and fall your bag
on the floor.You sat on the floor and cry out.You thought you can
trust your teacher but seems like nobody can be trusted.You cry
out even more after remembered that the say that 'the killer is
getting married'."I'm not a killer..I'm not a killer",you whisper
to yourself.
[Larry POV]
I walk in my office and people greet me normally.I sat on my
chair and a newspaper is already on my table,like they always
do.I read it while sipping my coffee.My eyes widened and I choke
on my coffee as I read the front page.I read the whole
article.Then,my phone started to rang."Why is Sharon  is on the
front page?And,wedding?How do people know about she's getting
married?She must be bragging about it.Ah!She doesn't have to tell
other people.What if people know that she's getting married to
me?Aish!She's so immature",I said to myself.
---------At school------
[Maddi POV]
"Yah,Lizzy,how did you know that Sharon is getting
married?",Chloe ask.I kept quiet.I didn't meant to hurt her that
way.I also got shock with the news.But,after thinking about what
she did 2 years ago,I couldn't forgive her.
"Maddi,are you okay?",Chloe ask.I smile and nod."Are you sure
with what you heard,Lizzy?",I ask her."Eum.",she replied with a
nod.
--------Flashback-------
"Yah!Maddi.I forgot my calculator.It's under my desk.Wait for
me,I want to take it",Lizzy said and walk back in the
school.After 6 minutes of waiting,she ran to me with a smile on
her face."You won't believe what I just heard",she said and look
at me and Chloe.

"What is it?",Chloe ask."That killer is getting married",she said.My eyes widened."Mwo?",I said to her."She told Mrs. Shim about it.I heard it just now.I was eavesdropping while walking to our class.I heard everything",she said to Chloe.I just kept listening to her without saying anything.
"Good.At least I have news to tell my dad.He could make it into front page.",Lizzy and Chloe laugh.
--------End of Flashback----


Chapter 10

[Larry POV]
I pick up my phone seeing my dad's id on it."Goodbye",I said while my eyes still sticks on tge newspaper."Pick up Sharon from school now.We need to talk about this immediately.Pick her up and take her to our usual restaurant",he said to me."Yes",I said and walk out of the office.
--------Reached School-----
I walk to the office and meet the principal."Who are you?",The principal ask me after I told him that I'll be picking Sharon up.I cannot tell him I'm her husband to be.So,I created a lie."I'm her father's assistant.Her father asked me to pick her up now.It's an emergency",I told him."Oh.It must be about the front page.She always creates trouble.",he shake his head."You have to see Mrs Shim.She's Sharon's homeroom teacher.",he said and show a table with a lady teacher.I nod and walk towards the teacher.
"Are you Mrs Shim?",I ask the lady.She raise her head and nod."Who are you?",she ask me."I'm Williams Sam's assistant.I'm here to take Williams Sharon.It's her father's order",I said.She nod showing that she understood."Please follow me",she said and walked out of the room.
"Somethig bothered her this morning.She came to me and start screaming.I don't know why she was screaming until I read the newspaper just now.",she explain whie we're walking to her classroom.
She open the door and I could see about only 20 students in there.Of course there's just a little number of students.It's only for rich kids."Where's Williams Sharon?",she asked the students."Nobody see her since this morning.She was never in",a girl said.I guess that's the class leader."No way!She came to me this morning",Mrs Shim said again."Well,that girl must be embrassed with her wedding.",a boy said and the whole class start laughing.
"Im Maddi .You're her friend,right?You must know we're she gone to",Mrs Shim said."Since when I'm her friend.I was never were her friend",she said.Mrs Shim walks out."I'm sorry.But I think she left school.Even her bag is not here.Maybe she went home already",Mrs Shim said.I nod and walk to my car."Where did this girl go?Aish!She's so annoying.First she tell everybody about the

wedding,now she's running away?What is running on her mind?",I
thought as I drive home.
~~~~~~~~
[Author POV]
You stood up after crying at the front door.You leave your bag on
the floor and start walking.You walk upstairs and went in the
store where all your old photos and stuff are kept.You close the
door and sat there quietly.It's so cold in there.You forgot to
turn on the heater.But you sat there and didn't even bother about
the coldness.
After half an hour,you start shivering.Your hand became numb.You
couldn't feel your finger.But tears still fell from your eyes.You
hope someone would come and calm you down.Hug you warmly.But you
know,nobody will come.You lie on the floor.You became
helpless.Your eyes closed.Trying to hold the coldness.You start
breathing heavily.
Then,you could feel someone pick you up bridal style.You try to
open your eyes but all you see is blurred images.You closed your
eyes again.You try to open your eyes again and saw him."Dear!You
came",you said with a slow voice.You see someone that you hope to
see,not the real one who pick you up.


                    Chapter 11


[Larry  POV]
I enter the house and saw Sharon's bag on the floor.I
frowned."She's here?",I thought to myself.
I went upstairs and walk to her room.She's nowhere to be
found."Sharon?!...Sharon ?!",I call her a few times.The house is
really cold.Even I start shivering.I look at the house's
thermostat and she didn't even turn on the heater.
I walk downstairs and walk till the back.I stop walking right
infront of the store.Suddenly,I have the urge to look in the
store.I walk towards it and open the door.My eyes widened.She lay
on the floor,shivering and sobs could be heard.I knelt down and
pick her up.
"Dear,you came",she said to me and smile.She expected me to
come?So,did she do this to get my attention?How could she?I can't
believe she's that kind of girl!
I walk to her room and put her down on her bed and pull up her
blanket."Dear,don't leave me!",she grab my hand and hold it.I
smirked.She doesn't even know me,but act like she's knew me for
years.So,she's really that kind of girl,huh?I pull my hand and
walk out.
I take my phone out of my pocket and call my dad."Dad,it seems
like I cannot bring Sharon to you.She's not feeling well",I
said.He sighed."Okay,we'll talk about this later",my father said
and kill the line.
----------At Night--------
[Author POV]

You open your eyes and sit up straight.You blink your eyes a few times to remember what happened.You stand up and walk out of your room.You walk downstairs and saw Larry is having his dinner. "I'm hungry",you said to him."So what?You want me to fix your dinner?You're old enough to take your own dinner right?Get it yourself",he said and continue munching.
He was angry because he thought that you announce about the wedding.Also,he thought that you're the kind of girl that wanted boys attention and flirty kind of girl.That's why he became cold towards you.
You turned your sight to the floor and walk to the fridge.You took out a pitcher of cold water and a glass.You pour the water and drink."Look at this.The front page of the paper is full with your picture.Also,if you turn on the tv,the news is all about the wedding.Do you really need to announce it?",he said.
"I didn't announce it",you said with tears in your eyes."But you must have tell somebody",he said.You look down and mumble to yourself."Yeah,someone who I thought I could trust".
You walk upstairs and tuck yourself into bed.You grab your phone and look at your wallpaper."I miss you,dear.Only you who knew I didn't do it.",you said and drifted to sleep.


Chapter 13


[Author POV]
You step in the house and go straight to your room.After you done changing,you walk back downstairs to drink some water.You didn't realise that Larry was sitting in front of the tv. You pour the water in your glass.
"I can't believe you're that stupid to believe people just like that.",he stand up behind you A few feet away.He fold his arm to his chest."What were you thinking?I thought you're old enough to be mature.",he said almost scream.You keep drinking the water after finish one glass because you're so thirsty.
"I also heard that you don't have any friends.I was wondering why but now I know why.Especially,after......the fire accident",he raise his brows.He actually don't know about the fire but after recalled what he heard outside the school,he try to provoke you with that.
You look infront of you with the glass in your hand.You raise your hand up high and smash the glass on the floor.You keep your poker face.The glass scattered all over the floor.A piece of it hit your leg and cause it to cut deep and blood flows out. Larry's eyes were widened.He saw the blood flow from your leg."Yah!...y....your.....leg",he stutter while his finger showing towards your leg."Don't worry.It's not painful at all.Compared to what you said just now",you chuckles and walk upstairs with the blood still flowing

Larry  was still in shock.He quickly take a mop and clean the whole glass pieces.
You went into your bedroom and grab a bandage and wrap your leg. Finish with it,you lie down and sleep.
~~~~~
[Larry POV]
I clean all the pieces and even make sure that none of the left.After that,I walk upstairs and got into my office room.I sat on my chair while thinking what I said that made her so angry.Was it about the fire?What is it about this fire?I look at my computer and start typing."SM Performance High School fire accident".
A lot of articles came up.I click one to read.I scroll down and keep reading about it.There was a picture of Sharon  for being the suspect for starting the fire.A person was killed.One of the students of the school.The investigation ended after Sharon confessed that she done it and the family of the victim forgive her."It can't be that easy.A girl killed their son but they forgive her?Something is not right here.",I said to myself.I scroll down even more and saw a picture of a guy."Richard",I read the name.He's the victim of the fire.
But,even reading the whole article is not complete.I need to know more about this fire accident.


                Chapter 14

[Author POV]
He was eating his breakfast on at the dining table,and saw you walk downstairs in your school uniform and bandage wrapped around your leg."You're not going to school today like that",he said and sip his coffee.You ignore him."Sharon !Listen to me.You're not going to school today!",he almost scream."Sharon!",you walk to the door and walk out.He sigh.
~~~~~~~~~
You find youself hard to walk properly since the cut was deep and hurts alot.You also didn't sleep properly last night.You walk slowly today.
Arrived at school,you ignore other people until the three girls came to disturb you."Oh,what happen to our bride-to-be?Did she hurt herself?Must be painful.",Lizzy said and mocked me."Not painful as my fist in your face",you thought to yourself.
~~~~During Class~~~~
[Larry POV]
I reached Sharon's school.I wanted to know what really happened about the fire accident.So,I decided to ask Mrs Shim about it.
I park my car and walk to teacher's room and walk to Mrs.Shim table.I bow."Mrs Shim,do you have time?I want to ask you about something",I said.She ask me to sit down and I did.
"What do you want to ask me,Mr...?",she ask."Brown.just call me Mr.Brown",I said and smile.
Purple-Mrs Shim,Blue-Larry

"I'm here to ask about the fire accident that happened here two years ago",
"I'm not sure if you're in the place to know about it.After all,you're just her father's assistant",
"It's what Sharon's husband-to-be wish.He wanted to know more about Sharon .Starting with her history",
"I thought you're her father's assistant",
"Yeah,but you know this whole family thing.It's bussiness.I'm not sure you'll understand."
"Fine.What do you need to know?",
"Did she really do it?Did she really started the fire?",
"I don't know.Actually nobody know about the truth whether she did or did not start the fire because nobody saw it.
"Then,why is she's the one who was accussed?If nobody saw her did it?",
"Firstly because she's the only one at scene during the fire.Second,because she was known as the one who clinging onto the victim.",
"What is the victim's relationship with Sharon?",
"Don't know.Some students said that she's really close with the victim.Some says that she's really like the victim even though the victim already had girlfriend.A few students hated her because they said that she is flirting with a guy that already had a girlfriend",
"You mean,the victim doesn't like Sharon ,but Sharon keep clinging on him?",
"You can say that",
"So,she kill the guy after the guy rejected her love?",
"She was accussed that way",
"Thank you.I think that's all I need to know",
"Can you help me?Please tell Sharon's husband-to-be to take care of her.She need support.I believed that she didn't do it.But there's nothing I can do to prove it",
"Ah!One last question.Why did the victim's parents let Sharon go?I mean,after she killed their son?",
 She almost explain but then a student ran to us and hold her hand."Mrs Shim..It's about Sharon!",she gasping for air after running."What about Sharon?",Mrs Shim asked.The girl raised her head."She fainted in the hall way"."Mrs Shim look at me.I quickly ran out and ran to the hall way.I saw a group of students gathered around her body,lying on the floor."Sharon !".I called her name.Blood flow through her bandage.I guess she's still in pain.I pick her up bridal style and walk to my car.


                    Chapter 15


[Author POV]
Arrived at the hospital,he quickly bring you to the emergency department."Help!..help!...somebody help me!...",he screams.A few

seconds later,3 nurse rushed to him and quickly put you on the bed and carry you to a room.
After an hour,a doctor walk out of your room.Larry  stand up and ask the doctor about you."How is she?",he asked."Her wound wasn't clean thoroughly.Bacteria catched up in the wound causes her fever.Thank god you bring her quick enough.Or not,her whole blood circulation could be affected.Don't worry.She's now asleep.I asked the nurse to clean her wound.",he said.Larry  bow to him and he walked away.
Larry walks to your room and saw the nurse left.He walk to you.He saw you still sleeping.He sat down on the chair placed next to your bed."What is your secret,Saron?",he whisper to himself. He fell asleep with his head next to your abdomen on the bed.
~~~~~Next Day~~~~
You slowly open your eyes.You tilt your head to the left side and saw he still sleeping.You frowned."Where am I?",you thought to yourself.You coughed a few times since you're fever still there.He woke up hearing your cough.He raise his head and look at you."Need anything?Water,maybe?",he said.
You shook your head."I want to go home now",you said and try to get off the bed."Ouch!",you almost scream as you try to move your leg."You're still not fully recovered.I'll take you home once the doctor said so",he said."I want to go home now!",you said as you get annoyed with him.
"What is your problem?Can't you just listen to me?I'm tired of hearing you screaming and demanding!I'm your husband-to-be!You have to respect me!",he said as he hold your shoulder.
"Let me go!I don't have to listen to you.I don't even want to marry you!!",you scream.He slapped you.You're eyes were widened.You were really shocked.You touch the cheek that he slapped.He quickly walk out of the room and leave you alone. He walked to the toilet and stare at his reflection in the mirror ."What have I done?",he ask himself."Oh my god!What have I done?",he said and sighed.He walk back to your room to apologize,when he saw you're no longer in the room. "Sharon!...Sharon !...",he call you a few times.But you're nowhere to be found.
~~~~~~
[Sharon POV]
I walk out the room as quickly as possible right after he left my room.I wear my school uniform and walk home.Eventhough the wound is really hurtful,I continue walking.I bear the pain alone. After 20 minutes of walking,I arrived at OUR house.I opened the door and walk to my room.I rest on my bed and slept cause I felt so tired.
~~~~~~
I opened my eyes when I realise I was sleeping for a long time.I woke up and it's already 6 pm.I wash up and wear my yellow pajama.I clean the wound and change into new bandage.I walk downstairs.I saw him having dinner.
"You never give me dinner or anything.And you call yourself husband?What a joke!",I said as I pour my water in my glass.I

heard his chair screech.Then,I felt a hand grab my shoulder and turned me around.His face was placed closed to mine.
He smirked."Isn't this what you want?Or you want me to change your bandage?You did that on purpose didn't you?",he said and laughed.I didn't really understand what he meant."What are you talking about?",I asked and frowned.
"You really did a great job to get my attention,Sharon .First,you ran away from school.And the best thing is that you knew I would come to you.I mean,"Dear,you came",that's the best acting I've ever seen.Then,you smashed the glass and cut yourself.I'm sure that you did it on purpose.Yesterday,you fainted at school,I mean,you knew that I was coming to your school.You're really great at this.",he smirked and fold his arm to his chest.
Tears collected in your eyes."You really think I'm that desperate,didn't you?",you said as you try to hold your tears."Isn't that the reason you start the fire two years ago?",he stated.Tears fell rolling on your cheek."I know everything about it.",he said and smile."No!You don't know the truth....you don't know the truth",you said and shook your head.You walk upstairs and keep shaking your head."You don't know the truth..I didn't do it".you said and walk to your room.You sat on your bed and hug your knees."I didn't do it",you keep repeating.


Chapter 16


[Larry POV]
Why do I feel so guilty.I mean,isn't it true?About what I said?She did that on purpose,right?Was I harsh towards her?
I walk upstairs to my bedroom.But,I felt so guilty,so I decided to check on her.Whether she's okay or not.I open her bedroom door slowly and saw she slept already.I walk in slowly and stand in front of her bed.I felt that I hate her,but at the same time,I felt gulity towards her.
I turn around and start walking when her phone,next to her was ringing.I quickly reach for it to stop the sound.It was a notification from her game that she was playing.I smiled.I want to put it down when I realise about her phone wallpaper.I look at it again.I frowned.
"I've seen this guy before.",I said to myself.Her wallpaper is a picture of her and a guy.They look so close together.She was smiling in that picture.I've never thought her smile would be beautiful.Since,I never seen her smiling before.But she looks happy with this guy.
I try to remember where I seen this guy before.I widened my eyes when it hit me.I quickly walk out of her room carrying her phone in my hand.I walk into my office room and sat in front of my computer.I type again what I typed about the fire accident."It

can't be him,is it?",I ask myself as I look at the articles
again.
I scroll down and keep scrolling till I saw his picture.Richard.I
reach for Sharon's phone and look at her wallpaper.They're the
same guy.I look again a few times.I'm 100% sure that they're the
same guy.I frowned and try to remember about what Mrs Shim told
me yesterday.
I'm really confused right now.I pull my hair a bit,trying to
think deeper."Why would he act as if he's happy being with her,if
he's not happy?.............Unless if he's really happy being
with her.",I widened my eyes.
"So,she's not clinging on the guy?...I'm really confused right
now!",I almost scream..


## Chapter 17-Explanation


For those who did not understand the last chapter,I will
explain...
I wrote that Larry  was going in internet about the fire
accident.So,he read an article.In the article,Larry  saw the
picture of Sharon  for being the suspect of the fire starter..and
also a picture of the victim who died in the accident.
The victim is a guy.Mrs.Shim told Larry  that Sharon  was
accussed for starting the fire with intention after the victim
reject her love.And the victim also hated her for being so
clinging on him.So,they're saying that Sharon was intentionally
wanted to kill the victim name Richard .
Then,on last chapter,Larry  enter Sharon's room and reach for her
phone to turn of the notification sound.But,he looked at Sharon's
wallpaper.
Sharon's wallpaper is a picture of her with a guy.In the
picture,Sharon  and the guy was smiling.So,Larry  thought that
she and the guy was close to each other.
But then,Larry  look at the guy and realised something.He thought
that he saw this guy somewhere.After thinking for a minute,he
realise that the guy in the wallpaper is the same as the guy in
the article.(the victim).So,he rushed to his office room and
search for the article again on the internet.
When he read the article again,he keep scrolling down and saw
again the picture of the victim.The guy in the picture in the
article is the same as the guy on Sharon's wallpaper.After he
look a few times,he was assured that the guy in the picture and
the guy on the wallpaper is the same person.


## Chapter 18

[Author POV]
You woke up remembering today is weekend.So,you won't have to go
to school today.You smile."At least I don't have to meet the

people there today",you said and stretch your body.You move your
have around the table next to you."Where is it?",you
thought.You're searching for your phone.You frown.You get off
your bed and start searching for your phone.
You walk out of your room slowly since your wound is not well
yet.Larry  was nowhere to be found."Could it be,he take it?But
why would he take it?",you thought to yourself.You walk to his
room.You knocked and open the door of his room.He was nowhere in
there.You frowned again.
You walk to his office room.You knock again,and open the door.You
saw him sleeping with his head on his arm,placed on the table.You
walk in and look around his table.You saw your phone placed in
his hand.You slowly reach for it and slowly pull it out from his
grab.
He move a bit which made you stop moving.You don't want to wake
him up.After he settle down again,you slowly pull it out.You bit
your lips,being nervous about him waking up in front of you.
When you already get your phone out,you felt relieved.You turn
around to the door when he move and start to wake up.You turn to
him again,hoping that he won't open his eyes.Not when you're in
his office.
But,you're wrong.He open his eyes and raise his head and saw you
standing in front of him.Your eyes widened.He flinched and sat
back.He was shocked to see you.He rub his eyes and open his
eyes."What are you doing here?",he ask.
"Why did you take my phone?",you ask with an innocent face.He
stop rubbing his eyes and start thinking for an
answer."Uhm......it was ringing last night.I thought that it
would disturb you.Since you need rest",he said and smiled.
You roll your eyes and walk out of his office.You walk in your
room and sat on the bed."Did he saw the wallpaper?",you ask
yourself.


                         Chapter 19


[Author POV]
You walk downstairs and saw Larry  eating his breakfast.He turn
around and saw standing at the stairs looking at him.He walk
towards you and teach for your hand."Come on.I prepare your
breakfast",he said and sat you down on a chair next to him."Why
suddenly?Is it about what I said before?You don't really need
to...",you said to him but he cut you."No.I want you taste my
cooking.",he said and put the french toast on your plate.
He look at you and smile."Eat",he said.You take the toast with
your hand and bite it and munch it."It's good",you said.He smile
and continue eating his toast."Sharon ,I want to ask you
something",he said.You look at him with an unpleasant
feeling."What is it;",you said.
"I want to know....about the fire accident",he said and look at
you.You stop munching immediately and stare at the plate.Your
hands start trembling.You blink your eyes a few time."I'm done

eating",you said and stand up and walk
upstairs."Sharon!....Sharon!",he call you.He sighed.
You walk in your room and sat on your bed."I need to get away
from him at the moment",you thought to yourself.You want to go
and shopping and do what girls usually do,but unfortunately you
don't have any friend.But,you thought of a place.So,you walk to
your bathroom to wash up.Finished,you wore a white dress with
floral print on it.
You walk downstairs hoping that Larry  is not there,but your hope
was useless.He was watching the tv.You have to pass the tv room
to make it to the door.You sigh.
He saw you standing."Eo,where are you going?",he ask.You kept
quiet.He stand up."Where are you going?",he ask again,now he
stand in front of you.Your eyes stare at the floor.He grab your
hand."If you won't tell me,then you cannot go out",he said."I'm
going out",you finally open your mouth."Where?",he ask and fold
his arm to his chest."Somewhere",you said."Then,you're not
going",he said and turn around to the tv room.
"You cannot do this to me!You cannot keep me in this house!",you
blurted out."Excuse me?You're the one who living in this house
like a living corpse and now you're blaming me?",he said
angrily."I try to understand you more,Sharon!",he added."By
asking me my history?About the fire accident?You want to know me
by knowing my history?If you want to know me by knowing about the
fire accident,then you won't understand me at all.By the way,who
are you to know about my past?",you said almost scream."Your
husband-to-be in 3 weeks",he said.Your blood boiling when you
heard that he said he's your husband to be."You slapped me before
and still admit to be my husband?YOU'RE IN NO PLACE TO KNOW MY
PAST!!",you screamed loudly,holding your tears.
You walk to the door and walk out of the house.He still standing
right where he was just now,still shocked with your scream.


                    Chapter 20

[Author POV]
You walk out of the house wondering where you should go.You
cannot turn back home after that fight just now.Then,you thought
of a place."I guess dad won't be at work today",you thought and
smile.
After walking for about 20 minutes,you arrived at home.You open
the door and enter."Dad!",you almost scream as you saw your
father sitting in the living room.He put down his newspaper and
look at you."Sharon?What you're doing here?",he stood up and
asked.You quickly hug him."I miss you",you said as you sniffing
his scent.He laughed."Ah!My daughter.But where's Larry?",he frown
as he ask the question.
You let off your hug and look at him."Why do you keep asking
about him when I'm around?",you ask and sat down on a couch."It's
just that he will be your husband",he said and sat across

you.Then,you heard a footstep going down the stairs.You look towards it and saw your mom.

She was shocked to see you."Mom!",you called.Her eyes widened."What are you doing here?",she said and frown."Can't I be home now?",you said."This is no longer your home,your house.Your house is with Larry.I knew I should have change the password of the door.",she said and make her way to the kitchen."What do you want this time?",she ask as she opening the refrigerator."I just wanna meet dad.That's all",you said with your innocent face."You met him already,right?Now go home.",she said.

"Why do you act like I'm not belong here?",you said as you stand up."Because you don't belong here!You belong to be with your husband now.You are now his responsible.And he is your responsible!!",she almost scream."HE'S NOT MY HUSBAND!!",you screamed."Yet",she said and raise her eyebrow.Your tears started to collect."Don't fight!This is my house and I will let anyone enter it if I want to.And you...",he look at your mother."Don't be harsh towards her.She still young",your father added. "That's your problem.You're spoiling her.Now look what happened",she said to your father.Your father walk upstairs to ease himself.Your mother look at you."Because of you,your parents fighting!Are you happy now?You shouldn't be back here.Don't return here!!",she scream.You reach for your bag and walk out with tears rolling on your cheek.

Chapter 21

[Author POV]
You stand at the outside and stare at the river.You thinking about your life."Accused to kill a guy,arrange marriage eith a guy you didn't even know,parents threw you out from their house.Your life is really blessed,Sharon",you said and chuckle. Tears fell.You start to sob."Deal with it,Sharon.There's nothing you can do about it!!",you scream towards the river.Then,you cry.Tears fell like river.You squat down and cry even more."What should I do?......what should I do?",you said softly while crying.
~~~~~
After some time,you calmed down and sat at the bench nearby.You just stare blankly.Then,your phone rang.You took it out from your bag and look at the caller id.It was Larry.You pick it . "What?",you said."Where are you?It's getting late.Come home now",he said.You don't know whether he's angry or not.But,you don't even care."Bye",you said and hung up.
~~~~~~~~~~
You reached home.You open the door and saw him standing a few feet away from you."Where have you been?",he ask."Somewhere",you said with no energy."Even toilet is somewhere.",he being sarcastic."Then,I went to toilet!!Happy?!!",you scream at him."You know you're not fully recovered.Why did you walk

out?What if something happen to you?",he said."Don't worry about
me.I've been living "alone" in this world for two years.So,you
just take care of yourself",you said and walk upstairs.You could
hear him sigh.
You enter your room and throw your bag on your bed with your
whole strength.Nobody know how much you wanted to scream your
heart out.You breath in and out.Then,you walk to your bathroom to
wash up.
After some time,you finish taking your bath and wear your pajama
and got ready to sleep.You close your eyes and you hear the sound
of your door being open."You don't want to eat dinner?",he
ask."Have you ever seen me eat dinner since I live in this
place?",you ask him.He sigh and closed the door again.


Chapter 22


You lock your door and sat on the floor.You back lean against the
door.Your eyes wander around.You breath heavily with your chest
out and in.Your panic attack came again.You had this since you
were traumatic with the fire accident.This trauma always attack
you if you dream about the fire accident.And last night,you
dreamed about it.You don't know where your pill is.You stand up
and search the while room.You pull out all your drawers from
their cabinet and all the content were spill out.You breath even
more heavily.It's like you lost your oxygen.You hold your chest.
You fell on the floor and you could hear Larry knock your
door.Sharon ,are you awake?",he ask.You try to call him.But,your
voice hardly come out."Help..".you helplessly call.You close your
eyes,hoping that someone would save you.You pass out.
[Larry POV]
I walk out of my room and walknpass her room.I heard things fell
off in her room.It was loud.I wonder what she was doing in
there.After everything was quiet,I decided to knock her door.I
could hear a whisper but that was it.I try to open her door but
it was locked.I quickly ran to my office room and grab the keys
for the rooms in the house.I walk to her room again and open the
door after unlock it.
I was shocked to see Sharon lying on the floor.All of her drawers
was  taken out from their cabinets and all the contents were
scattered all over the floor.It's like she was robbed or
something.I walk to her and shake her body."Sharon!....Sharon!",I
call her hoping that she would open her eyes.
I take her phone from the bed and dialled her father's
number."What is it?",he said as soon as he pick up the
phone."Mr.Williams?It's me,Lawrence.I want to ask you if Sharon
have a private doctor or something?",I said."Did she fainted?",he
ask."Yeah",I said."Call Dr.Lee.It's available in her contact",he
said.I quickly hung up and search for Dr.Lee in her contact.
~~~~~~

"Here.I don't know how she could lost her pills but I'll give you new bottle of it.She knows how to take it.Just call me if you have any question",the doctor said.I nod and send him out till the door.I look at the bottle in my hand."Trauma attack?",I ask myself.

I walk up to her room and take her phone with me.And I walk to my office room and sat on the chair.I put the phone on the table and look at the bottle of pills."If she started the fire,why would she have trauma attack?She do it intentionally",I thought to myself.

I put the bottle on the table and grab the phone.I unlock it and look at the wallpaper.Actually,I was staring at it.I really don't know what to think about this fire accident thing.The only way I would know the truth is by story from her own mouth.


## Chapter 23


You sat on your bed after you woke up from passed out.You were scared.Really scared.Your past haunt you again.It's been a while since you dream about the fire accident.But,now you had them again."It's all because of him.If he didn't ask me about it,I won't dream about it.",you said to yourself.Then,you lose control of your body.

You stand up from your bed and walk downstairs.You head towards the kitchen.You look around and saw what you want.Knives.You grab one and walk slowly back upstairs.

You walk like a woman who possesed by a ghost.You walk towards his office room and open the door.You saw him sleeping with his head on the table.You walk towards him slowly.You stop right in front of him.You grin."I won't suffer anymore",you said.You hold the knife up with the blade towards down and aim at Larry who still sleeping.

"I'm sorry",you whisper.He heard a voice.He open his eyes and quickly look up and his eyes saw you standing in front of him with a knife in your hand.He quickly move away when you try to stab him."Sharon,stop!",he said as he fell on the floor from his chair."You!! If only you didn't ask about it,I would let it go",you scream.Larry  was flustered."Sharon!Calm down.You're not in your right mind",he said as he stand up."I lost my mind two years ago.",you said.Tears fell from your eyes...

"People call me a killer eventhough I'm not.But today,I will be a killer.If I don't get to kill you.....",you said and sobs."Then,I'll kill myself",you add and hold the knife to your neck.

"Sharon!Calm down.Please",he beg you.You keep crying."I can't live like this anymore",you said and move your hand to cut your neck but he quickly reached for your hand and throw the knife away.You both struggled.You struggled to reach for the knife while he struggle to throw the knife farther.

When you reached the knife,he grab it from you.But he holds at
the blade causes his hand to bleed.He try his hard to get it away
from your hand.Blood starts to flow more and more.But he ignore
the pain.He gain his strength and with one move,he  success in
throwing away the knife.He walk to you and slapped you again.You
were shocked.
Finally,your sense came again.You look at him.And look at his
palm."What have I done?",you saw his palm bleeding."I'm sorry.I'm
so sorry",you said."It's okay.I'll just wrap it with some bandage
and it'll be fine.",he said."No!I'll do it",you said and quickly
walk to your room to take a first aid kit.Then,you walk back to
his office."Let's go to your room.",you hold his wrist and bring
him to his room.
"Sit down",you order him.He sat down on his bed.You sat next to
him.You took out the things you need to clean his palm.
He look at you.You head slowly get lower while your hand still
moving.He try to look at your face but you block his view by
lowering your head.He then feel tears fell on his palm that
you're cleaning.You sob slowly.
"Don't cry.",he said as he hold you chin and raise your head.He
saw your eyes were red and it was swollen.You look at him."Can't
you tell me what happened?",he said softly.


Chapter 24


"I don't know if I should tell you or not.",you hesitated.He hold
your hand."Just tell me,please",he said.You look at his face.You
wonder whether it's his honest face or not.
"Fine",you sigh."I met this guy.He was my senior.I still remember
his first sentence to me.He asked for my name and my class.He's
the first guy that talked to me on my first day of school.It was
interesting.So,I try to know him more.I found out his
name.Richard.Everytime he saw me,he would smile to me.I fell in
love.I didn't know that he too liked me.But,we just continue that
kind of relationship.",you smile as you remember back.
"But I heard that he already had a girlfriend",Larry ask you."I
am his girlfriend that everyone been saying about.He decided to
keep our relationship as a secret.He has a reputation to keep.He
is our school's best student.That's why nobody knew about our
relationship.But they keep saying that I was flirting with
him.",you said.
"Then,what about the fire?",Larry  ask again."I really didn't
know anything about it.That day,our school had class till 9 pm
because exam is coming.So,that night I walk to the toilet
alone.That night,only the first class will study till 9pm.Other
class' students all went home.".you explain.
You frown as you try to remember every detail."I went to toilet
alone.Then,I saw this orange reddish light from outside of the
toilet's window.I was wondering what it was.So,after I finish

cleaning my hands,I walk out and went behind the toilet
building.Behind the toilet building was a store where the janitor
put all the planting stuff.But,it was burning.I was shocked.I
thought that there's nobody in there so,I thought that I should
leave.But,I heard a guy's voice calling for help with a slow
voice.He sounds so helpless",your tears fell.
"I called for help.But there's nobody there.Also,my class was
far.I cried while looking around searching for anything that
could help him.But,I was to shocked and frightened,my mind wasn't
working at that time.I end up standing and my body was
shivering,still shocked.After some time,the janitor came.He saw
me standing and looked at the store,it burned.He start
screaming.Then,all the teachers came and saw me.I was to shocked
to explain what happen.I wasn't crying,I didn't scream for help.I
just stand there with my widened eyes.",you said and sobs could
be heard."You don't know how I felt,seeing him,burned,asking for
my help,but I didn't do it.I didn't help him.",you shook your
head and tears keep falling."Since that day,I was called as a
killer.People said I'm the one who did it",you continue.
"I couldn't sleep for the whole 1 year.Regretting that I didn't
save him from the fire",you're done with cleaning Larry's
hand.You stand up and reach for the bandage to wrap it around
Larry's hand.Why didn't you fight in court?Stand for yourself",he
ask."I did.I lost",you answer."But the truth always win in
court",Larry said.You chuckle while wrapping his
hand."Truth?Truth doesn't win in court.What won,that's the
truth.Even though it's wrong,if it win in court,it will be
counted as the truth.And everyone will believe it.",you said to
him.


Chapter 25


You woke up remembering it's school today.You were
late."Aish!!",you screamed as you look at your clock.Larry heard
your scream and smiled.He knew you were late.
"Lawrence,why didn't you wake me up?Now I'm late",you said as you
run downstairs."I'll send you then",he said."No,it's okay.I don't
want to trouble you",you said as you slip in your shoes."Let me
send you",he hold your hand and look at you.You nod.
~~In Car~~
"That's the first time you called me my name.I started to think
that you don't even know my name",he said."What?",you said and
start remember that you called his name this morning."Ah...",you
said and smile of embarassement."I like the way you call my
name.But,you can call me Larry.",he said."Larry?",you look at
him."It's what my friends called me.Since you'll be my wife,you
should call me that too",he explain."Larry",you said softly and
smile.

~~~~~~~
Reached at school,you get out of the car.He too."Lawrence,get in
the car.People will see you with me.Get in the car",you said as
you try to cover your face.You were scared that you will
embarrass him."It's okay.You'll be my wife anyway.",he said and
smile."And call me Larry",he added."Fine.Now go before anyone
sees you",you start to walk.He grab your hand and pull you.You
turn to him.And he did something that shocked you.
He Kiss Your Lip.
Your eyes widened.After he let go,he smiled"Thanks for believe in
me the other day",he said.You were still shock with his kiss.You
turn around and walk with your widened eyes.
U walk to your locker.You open it and put the books in your
bag.Then,your hand stop moving and you stare blankly.You were
flashed with the picture of him kissing you.
Without you knowing,........
YOU SMILED


                        Chapter 26



--------Finished School------
You decided to visit your father at his office.Since your mother
doesn't like you to come to her house.You walk to your father's
company.
After 20 minutes of walking,you reached his company .You
naturally walking in the building since everyone knew who you
are.You walk in the elevator and pressed the level button.After
some time,you heard a 'ding' sound indicates you arrive to level
you wanted.
You walk towards his office and pass his secretary."Is dad
inside?",you ask his secretary.She nodded and you smiled
automatically.
You open his office door and step inside."Dad!",you call him
excitedly then you saw a familiar figure sitting next to him.
Larry.
You were shocked.He smile at you."Oh?How did you know that
Lawrence was meeting me?Did you call her?",your father said and
asked Larry.He shook his head showing that he did not call."I
thought that I want to visit you.But looks like you are
busy.So,I'll go",you said and turn around when your father
said."It's okay.We're talking about you just now",he said."Am I
in trouble?",you ask with your innocent face.
"Sit down,baby girl",your father call you.You sat accross
him."What is it about?",you ask.You look at Larry  and he smile
at you."Lawrence  gave me a great idea",your father said.You look
at him again."What idea?",you ask Larry.
"I thought that maybe we should make our wedding faster.I
mean,it's in two weeks time but,living together without any bond

is kind of awkward.So,I try to ask dad about it.And he seems to agree with me.",Larry explain.
You try to object his idea but when you thought of his kiss this morning,you stopped."Maybe this is the happiness that you've been searching for,Sharon",you thought to yourself.
"What do you think?",your father ask you.You nod showing that you agree."Then,we'll be having a wedding celebration this end of the week",your father said loudly and laughed.Larry smile of happiness.

~~~~~~In Car~~~~~~

-----------SILENT----------

Then he opens his mouth."Thank you for accepting my idea",he said."But why didn't you said anything to me...about the wedding thing",you said softly."Sorry.I just thought about it after I sent you to the school",he explain.You just nod.
Then,Silent crept again.......
You both reached house at night since you guys had dinner with your father.
Finished taking your bath,you wrapped yourself with your towel.You open the door and scream loudly.Larry  was standing a few step away from you.You try to cover yourself."Sorry.Sorry",he said and turn around.When you're sure that he wasn't looking,you get out from the bathroom quickly and reached for your pajama.
"I just wanted to say thank you.",he said.You stopped moving.You can't believe he said that."Thank you for accepting my proposal just now",he said.Finish wearing your pajama you ask him to turn around.He took a small towel on your bed and start drying your hair.You were still shock with his move."Aih...My wife is beautiful",he said as he still drying your hair.Slowly smile crept on your face.
"Larry",you call him."What is it?",he said."The kiss,....you gave me this morning"you said."What's wrong with it?",he ask.His hand still moving."Thank you for that.It's my first kiss",you said.His hand stop moving.The smile on your face dissapear.
He holds your chin and raise your face to his.And another chup.....
He Kiss You Again..


                    Chapter 27


-----------Skip To Wedding--------
You stand in front of a mirror in the waiting room.You look at your reflection.Your chest move in and out.You breath in and out.Trying to shake off the nervous.Then,someone enter the room.You turn back and saw your mom walk in."Wah,our daughter is really beautiful",she said and hug you.You smile."At last,I felt so relieved",she added."What do you mean?",you ask."Well,from now on,you're not our responsible anymore.So,your father doesn't have to think about you too much.I hope you don't make Lawrence

burdened.He's a good guy.Be a smart wife,okay?",she laugh and
walk out of the room.
"Am I a burden?",you look up.Hoping that you would get the
answer.You sigh.You sat on a chair and you keep worrying."What if
I am a burden?",you ask yourself.Then,a knock could be heard on
the door.The wedding planner open the door."Please get ready",she
said.You nod.You follow her to the hall.
Your wedding is a private wedding.So only family and friends will
come.But,you don't have any friends.You fold your arms with your
father and he guide you through the aisle.
"Sharon ,be a good wife.Be loyal to your husband.Don't make him
sad.Be with him whenever he need someone.I don't know how much
time I have left to be in this world.",your father whisper to you
as you were walking the aisle.Tears collected in your
eyes."Dad,don't say like that",you hold your tears.
Actually your father has a secret but he told no one about it.
You raise your head and saw Larry looking at you.Smiling from ear
to ear.You lower your head again to hide the tears in your eyes.
Reached at Larry,your father let go of your arm and put your hand
on Larry's hand."Please take care of my daughter",he
said."What,Father",he said and look at you."You look
beautiful",he said.You blushed.
"Can we start?",the priest said.
~~~~~~~~~~~~~~
Done with the wedding,Larry  stand next to you."Are you
ready?",he asked."Ready for what?",you said innocently.He came
close to you."Our.........honeymoon",he said and chuckles."We're
going to Paris.City of love",he said and hold your hand."When are
we going?",you ask him."Tonight.But the airport is quite far,so
we have to move early",he said.You nodded.
"Dad.Dad have to take care of your health.Dad cannot skip your
meal.I won't visit you as much as now.If Dad miss me,just call
me.I'll come,okay?",you said as you try to hold your tears.
Your father kiss your forehead."Now go.Search for the happiness
that you lost for 2 years",he said and smiled.Tears fell from
your eyes and roll down on your cheek.Larry was standing at your
back,a few feet away."Larry,take care of my daughter.Don't make
her cry,okay?",your father said to him.He bow to your father and
smiled."I will,father",he replied.


                         Chapter 28

You guys sat in the airplane side by side.You were shivering
because the air-con was so cold.He look at you and smiled.He then
opened his bag and lend you a blanket."Here,wear this",he
said.You shook your head."No need.I can handle it",you said while
hugging yourself.He unfold the blanket and cover your body with
it."From now on,listen to me.I'm your husband",he said.You look
at him.You were confused whether he's angry or not.
"Larry,can you change place with me?I want to sit next to the
window",you said."Of course",he said.Your seat were big and

private since your seat were in first class."But it's dark out there",he said."It's okay.I like to sit next to window.",you said and smile.

Afer an hour,your eyes slowly closing.He turn to you and saw you sleeping.He smile seeing you look cute while sleeping.He pull the blanket up to your chin and slowly,he kiss your lips.He ,then close his eyes and sleep.

~~~~~~~~~~~

After a few hours,you feel your body was shaken.You open your eyes and saw Larry  in front of you."We're here",he said.You look out the window and saw clouds and land.You smile."Don't you want to fix your makeup?",he said.You touch your face."Do I look bad?",you asked."You look beautiful for me is already enough",he said and smiled.You blushed.

He hold your hand slowly walk out of the airport."Where should we go now?",he ask."Why don't we go to hotel first.I'm tired.",you said."Okay",he said.He hold a taxi and you guys went to hotel.

~~~~~~~~~~

Arrived at the hotel,he took the luggage out of the boot of the taxi and paid the taxi driver.You walk in the hotel together.He then,walk to the receptionist and check your name for your reservation.

After a few minutes,you got a suite for yourselves.You were really excited.You walk to the elevator and pressed the level 8.Inside the elevator,he hold your hand."Where should we go after this?",he ask."Let's grab something to eat",you said.He nod. Reached your room,he scan the card on the door and open it.You step in and your mouth automatically open wide."It's so big",you said.While he stand behind you,a few feet away and smile seeing you're happy.

He walk towards you and backhugged you.You flinched but he hold you tight."From now on,let's be happy,okay?",he whisper in your ear.You smile.

You lie down on the bed and later,he lie next to you.You rest your head on his arm."I'm tired",you said softly."Sleep then.When you wake up,we'll go out and have dinner,okay?",he said.You nod.You close your eyes and drifted to sleep.

~~~~~~~~

You open your eyes and saw Larry still sleeping next to you.You look at his arm.It was red."It's must be hurtful",you said to yourself.You move your hand to his shoulder."Larry ,wake up.It's already dark",you said.He open his eyes and rub it a few times. "Let's go have dinner",he said and got out of the bed.He took off his shirt in front of you.You look down,feeling embarassed.You got out of the bed and wall to the bathroom and fix your makeup.


Chapter 29


You both got back from dinner."I'll shower first since I'm tired",you said to him."Don't be too long.I'll shower after",he said.You nod.You reached for your towel and pajama and walk in the bathroom.

After some time,you walk out of the bathroom and see him only in towel covering his lower part.You quickly turn around and act like nothing happen.He didn't saw you turn around,so he just walk in bathroom.

Your heart beat so fast.You try to control the pace but then,you were worried."Where should I sleep tonight?",you said softly."I can't sleep on the same bed as him",you add.You sighed.

You sat on the edge of the bed while drying your hair.Finished with shower,he walk out of bathroom.He saw your face looks like you're worried.

"Is something wrong?",he ask.You raise your head and look at him.You shook your head.You stand up and stand in front of the window,looking at the view outside.

Then,you `felt he backhugged you.You slowly put down your towel,let it fall on the floor.This is what you've been worrying about.Wedding Night.

He backhug you and his face buried in your neck.You could feel him kissing you and bit your skin softly.You whimper Larry",you call him with lust.

Then,his hand quickly turn you around and he kiss your lips deeply.He then bit your lip,asking for entrance.You parted your lips and his tongue dancing with yours.You moan slowly.You wrapped your arms around his neck while his hand wrapped around your waist.

He push you slowly to bed.Then,he got on top of you without breaking the kiss.His hand unbottoned your pajama and throw it away to the side.He also pull off your pants leaving you in your bra and panty.You try to cover yourself but he stop you.

He then kiss your jaw to your collar bone,trail to your cleavage.He lean on the headboard of the bed and you sat on him.He look in your eyes,full with lust.He ran his finger on your shoulder and slowly pull down your bra lace until your breast fall out from it.He then came close to your breast and suck it.You wrapped you hand around his head and pull him closer so he would go deeper while your lower part keep rubbing his clothed cock.He wrapped his hand around your waist and suck your breast even more.

You moan softly.He then let go of your breast and do the same to your other breast.You could feel that you were getting wetter down there."La.....Larry".you call him.He keep sucking your breast.He then finish with your breast,he remove his towel releasing his member standing.He pull your body to sit on him but before he slide it in you,you stop him.

You look him in the eyes."I'm scared".you said softly."Don't worry,it'll hurt first,but the pain will go away",he asure you.You saw honesty in his eyes.Then,you nod.

You remove your panty and he slowly slide it in your inferior part.You almost scream,but you hold it.Tears fell.He wipe your tears with his thumb.You hug him while moving up and down.And your pace become quickly.You both let a messy moans.

After some time,you both let out the juices.You lie down next to him and he hug you and kiss your temple.


Chapter 30

You open your eyes.You squint your eyes and look Larry was sleeping next to you.You slowly sat up and realise you're not wearing anything.You look at your body.You were naked and you only cover your body with blanket.You saw bloods on the blanket also.Your eyes widened.Then...

You scream......loudly.
Larry  was shocked.He quickly open his eyes and because of panicked,he lost control of his body and fell from the bed.You cover your mouth with your palm.You look at Larry with your widened eyes."YOU DID THIS TO ME!!",you said while tears fell.You still cannot believe you don't have virginity anymore.
"Sharon,calm down",he said.He stand up from the floor and he's also naked.You quickly shut your eyes and look away.You keep crying."What did you do to me last night",you ask.He laughed."Come on.It's not like I raped you or something",he said and lean his head on your shoulder."Stop crying",he said and wipe your tears with his thumb.You stop crying."It hurts",you whimper and look at him.He put his warm hand on your belly and slowly massage it."Better?",he ask.You nod.
"Come on.There's still a lot that we need to do today",he said and walk to the bathroom."Such as?",you ask."SHOPPING!!!",he said.You smiled.
~~~~~~~~~~~~
"Larry.I want that!",you show him a bikini set.You actually don't want it.It's just that you wanted to see him if he give you permission to wear something sexy."No!",he shake his head and continue scooping his ice-cream in a cup."Why not?",you ask and pouted."I'll buy it for you if you only use it for me",he said.You smile."He do care about me",you thought to yourself and smiled.
You both enter a jewelry shop.You set your eyes on a beautiful bracelet.Charm bracelet."You want it?",he ask you.He saw you keep staring at the bracelet."Can I?",you look at him.He nodded.And he did bought you the bracelet.
You both keep walking till you reach a place.There were a lot of people around there.Yoi were curious about what happen there.You saw a woman,a tourist standing near you.So,you decided to ask her."What's happening there?",you ask her."Oh,it's a water fountain.It is believed that if you wish and throw a coin in there,your wish will come true",she explain to you.You were interested.
You turn around and grab Larry's hand and walk near the water fountain.You saw people close their eyes and throw coins in there.You quickly take out a change in your pocket.Chen saw

you."You really believe in those things?",he asked.You look at
him.Your face turn into a sad face.Larry thought you were going
to cry."Okay,okay.Let's do it",he said and take the coin from
your hand.He close his eyes and smiled.Then,he throw the coin in
the fountain."My turn",you said.You make your hand into a ball
and raised your hand up to your chin level.You close your eyes
and wish.You smile.You took a quite long time to wish.After
that,you open your eyes and throw the coin.
~~~~~~~~
On the way to the hotel,the weather was cold and it's night
already.You put your hands in your pocket."What did you wish for
just now?",he ask."It's a secret.I cannot tell",you smile as you
were thinking about your wish."I'm your husband,you have to tell
me.",he said.You shake your head."Fine,then walk alone",he got
sulky.He was actually joking but you thought he was really
angry.You stopped your movement.He was walking quickly to the
front,leaving you behind.
Tears collected in your eyes.He turn around and saw you just
standing there,looking at him with your teary eyes."Sharon ,I was
joking",he said and walk towards you.You started to cry slowly.He
hold your arms but you push his hand.You start walk quickly,still
crying."Sharon !",he called you.You sobs.He quickly ran towards
you and backhugged you."I'm sorry",he whispered."Don't ever leave
me.There's too many people left me.I don't want you to leave me
too",you said trying to hold your tears."Okay.I won't leave
you",he said.You were still traumatic about people leaving
you.It's still sensitive to you.
He turn you around,facing him."Now stop crying,you look ugly.",he
said while wiping your tears and chuckled.He hold your head and
kissed your forehead."Now come on.It's getting colder out
here",he said.He pull your hand out of your pocket and hold it
along the walking.
~~~~~~~~~~~~
Reached hotel,you both take your shower.Finish your shower,you
both sat on the bed,watching tv.Suddenly,you ask him a
question."Do you think the room cleaner know what we've done last
night?",you ask him.He look at you."I mean,she changed the bed's
cover.So,she must have known what we've done last night",you
said."It's what all honeymoon couple do.It's normal",he said with
his poker face.
He look at you."Are you still angry?",he ask.You nod."Then,let me
make you forgive me",he said and came close to you.He then kiss
your lips.You too,reply his kiss.
And you did it that night.


Chapter 31

--------After One Week of Honeymoon--------
"Larry,I'm so tired right now",you said to him ."Okay.After
this,we go home and rest okay?",he said while reading magazine in

the plane.You look outside the window with a boring look."Sharon
,you haven't Vix,right?",ask while his eyes still on the
magazine."Who's Vix?",you ask him."My friends",he replied."Those
dozens of boys at our wedding?",you ask him with your eyes
widened.He nod."You don't know them,right?",he ask.You nod."I'll
introduce them later to you",he said.
"But why are there so many of them?",you ask him."I'll explain
later.Go to sleep.You must be really tired",he said.You nod and
close your eyes.He put a blanket on your body and kissed you.
~~~~~~~~~~~
"Sharon....Sharon....wake up.We're here already",he said waking
you up.You open your eyes and fix your hair.He hold your hand and
help you with your bag.You still in your sleepy mode,just follow
him wherever he lead you to.
After collected your bag,you walk outside the airport.You saw
Larry calling someone to pick you up.You were really sleepy.Larry
look at you and smiled."My wife is so cute when sleepy.Here,hop
on my back.Sleep on my back",he knelt down.He piggyback you.You
sleep with your head on his shoulder."Where is this driver?What
took him so long?",he thought to himself.People around just look
at him in a weird way.People thought that he is carrying a drunk
woman.
After 2 hours of waiting,the driver arrived.He put you down on
your feet and slide you at the back seat.He ask the driver to put
the luggage in the boot of the car.He sat next to the driver.
"What took you so long?",he ask the driver while massaging his
shoulder."Sorry,sir.It was a traffic jam.",the driver
answer.Larry turn and look at you sleeping peacefully.
5 minutes later,you woke up.You sat up straight.You saw Larry
still massaging his shoulder."Larry,does it hurt?",you ask and
massage him."Oh,a bit",he said."OMG.I was so sleepy.",you said
.He smile."Here,let me massage it for you",you said.
Arrived at your house,you open the door and walk straight to your
room."I'm so tired right now",you said."I'll shower then",you
said."Me too".he said and joined you."No!".you stop him in front
of the bathroom."Showering together is not allowed",you said to
him.He lean on the door and fold his arm to his chest."Well Mrs
Brown Sharon,please be inform that this is my house,and I can do
anything in it",he said with his eyebrow raised."Anything?",you
said."Anything",he reply and carry you bridal style and brought
you inside the bathroom.
~~~~~~~~~~
You were wearing a couple pajama with Larry.You lie down on your
bed and he came later.He lie next to you and slowly,he pull you
into his embrace.He whisper in your ear."Sharon,next time.Call me
dear",he said."Hmm",you hummed.You were too tired to reply to
him.He look at you and kiss your cheek.He hugs you tight and
drifted to sleep

Chapter 32

You open your eyes seeing that you're alone on the bed.You look around while scratching your head."Larry",you call slowly.He's not around.You got off the bed and walk downstairs.You smell something good.You smile.You quickly ran downstairs and saw Larry in the kitchen cooking something."What are you cooking?",you ask him.He smile."No morning kiss?",he ask while his eyes still on the food he's cooking.You shook your head."You left me alone on the bed.So no morning kiss for you.I only give morning kiss on bed",you said and walk towards the dining table.

You sat on the chair and suddenly Larry's phone on the table was ringing. Larry,your phone is ringing",you said and he quickly walk towards you.He grab his phone and walk outside and walk upstairs.You were wondering who's he talking to.But you walk towards the stove to continue cooking Larry's pancake."Wah..it's pancake",you said and smile.

---------While Larry--------

"Hello",he said."Sir,I've search about the fire.The case that you asked me to investigate.But,there's not too much information that we can get since only a few people involve in it.Only the people in school knows about the accident",the guy on the other line said."What about Richard's friends?Classmates?Maybe they know something.Find the informations that I need.I want full report on our meeting tommorow",Larry said."Yes sir",the guy replied.He then kill the line.

Larry  actually hired a private investigator to investigate your case.He couldn't let you live in guilty anymore.He want to make sure his wife's name is not damaged and called as a killer.He wanted to do the right thing.

He walk back down and saw you already ate all of the pancake that he cooked."Where's my share?",he ask as he sat across you.You stop munching.You look at him with your widened eyes.Your mouth is full with the pancake."OMG,it's just that it was so delicious.",you said with a cute face.He smiled."Since when you eat so much?",he said to you.You push your plate towards him and walk away.He was shocked with your attitude.


Chapter 33


You sat next to Larry with your head on his shoulder."Larry",you call him."I told you to call me dear right?",he said while his eyes stick on the tv."Fine.Dear..Can you do me a favor?",you ask him."What?",he said."Promise me you'll do it first",you said and shake his arm."Ok,I promise.What is it that my wife wants?",he ask."I want...........strawberry",you said with a big smile."What?",he said loudly with his eyes looking at you.You frown."You promised me",you said with a bit angry."But......but.....w-where sh-should I buy it?It's late now",he said."I don't care.Just buy it.You promised me",you scream at him and hit him with a small pillow.He sighed.

~~~~~~~~~~~~

He walk down the way to market try to find strawberry for you.He keep blowing in his palm trying to keep warm while cold wind hit him."Strawberry......straberry.....where should I buy strawberry....",he start singing softly."No...This is too much.Asking me to buy strawberry in the late night.How could she...?",he started to get angry."But,suddenly asking for food in the middle of the night?She never do this before?Is she.....??..........Nah",Larry shake his head and continue walking.

He reached to a small roadside shop with an old woman in it.The woman is closing her shop."Excuse me,madam...Can you please give me strawberry?Take away",Larry said while blowing in his palm."Sorry son,but I'm closing right now",the woman said."Please..it's for my wife",Larry  said and look at the woman in her eyes.The woman suddenly smiled."Ahhh.....for two?",she smiled."She's so lucky to have you?",she added."What?",Larry  was shock with what she said just now.

-------Reached Home------

"Done it.",you said with a cranky tone."Shouldn't you be sleeping right now?You have school tommorow ,missy",he said while plating your strawberry."It's Mrs now.I want to eat it",you said.He put the plate in front of you and sat across you."Is it good?",he ask.You nod your head."Here",you gave him one piece.He open his mouth and ate it."Oh,it's good.Give me some more",he said.You shake your head."It's for me,so I'll eat it",you said while putting another piece in your mouth."I bought it.It's cold outside but I still bought it for you",he said with his eyes widened.He start to pull the plate towards him."No",you said and pull back the plate.

Finish the strawberry,you walk upstairs and lie on the bed."You cannot sleep now.Or not you'll get fat.",he said while turning off the light."You don't love me if I'm fat?",you sat on the bed while he lie down."Who would love a fat wife?",he jokes.You grab your blanket and got off the bed."I'll sleep in MY room then",you said and walk out.He laugh.

You lie on your bed in your room.Then,you saw him enter your room."I'm sorry.I was just joking around",he said."That's not funny,dear"you replied."Fine,I'm sorry",he said and lie next to you.He hugs you tightly.

"Dear,can I ask you something?",you said and look at him."What?",he ask with his eyes closed."If one day,I'm.....I'm...pregnant,maybe someday,will you accept the baby?",you ask.He open his eyes and look at you."Of course.I will make sure nothing happens to you or the baby.If something happens to the baby,I will not forgive myself for not taking care of you.But,I'm sure nothing's going to happen.Why suddenly you ask this question?",he ask you.You hug him around his waist and put your head on his chest."Just asking.So that I know you'll love our baby.It's such a relief listening you said that.But,we're not having baby's before I graduate my school",you said and hit him lightly on his chest."Okay",he smiled

He send you to school."You want me to pick you up later?",he ask you.You shake your head."No need.I don't want to trouble you.",you said and kiss him.You open the door and walk in the school.You walk to your locker and as usual you open the locker and take your stuff.

Suddenly,you felt this weird feel.You quickly close your mouth and ran to the nearest toilet.You open the door and ran to one of the room.You throw up in the bowl.Finish throwing up,you frown."It must be because I ate last night",you said while rubbing your stomach.

You wash your hand and walk back to your locker.Then,you felt dizzy and it hurts so much.You hold your head.You grab your bag and walk to the teacher's room.Then,suddenly you have the urge to throw up again.You quickly ran back to the nearest toilet.You threw up again.

You frown.You look at the reflection of yourself in the mirror."Am I really that fat?",you said.You turn your body around.You grab your bag and walk to the teachers room.

You meet Mrs Shim."Teacher,can I take a day off today?",you sat in front of her."Mia,you already take 2 weeks of day off.Kids already trying to figure out why you were off.I already give you two weeks for your wedding.",she said with a slow tone.

"But I kept throwing up and now I felt really dizzy",you said to her.Her eyes widened."Did you.........do it?",she ask."Do what?",you look at her."You know......the S word",she said.Your eyes widened."Ah...Sharon!",she screamed.You were shocked."Go home.Now!....and go to the nearest pharmacy and buy the pregnancy tester",she said in slow tone and quick.

You quickly walk out of school and walk home."Pregnancy tester?What should I do with it?I'm not......pregnant right?",you said while rubbing your tummy."No way",you shake your head.

After walking for 5 minutes,you reach to a pharmacy."Should I enter?",you ask yourself.You just push the door open and walk in.A lady walks to you."How can I help you",she ask with a smile."Ah....haha....",you chuckles shyly.You don't know how to explain.

"Do you have that pregnancy tester?",you said shyly."Ah..Follow me",she said and you follow her."We have a few brands here,but I suggest you use this.It's easier to understand",she said.You nodded."I'll take that then",you said.She take the box and put it in a plastic bag.

You take the box and put it in your bag.You look at the lady just now."You're not judging me in your head right?",you ask her."No.We always have pregnant student came to buy that.So,it's kinda normal",she explain.You nod.

--------Reached Home--------

You look at the box."Should I really use this?I'm too young to use this.",you sigh looking at the box."I'll just use it

tommorow.",you said and put it back in your bag.You lie down on
your bed cause you still feel dizzy.
--------At Night-------
"Sharon ,why aren't you at school just now?I searched for you all
over the place",Larry said right after he enter the room.He got
angry cause he searched for you from the time of school ended
till night."I told you,you don't have to pick me up",you were
angry.You sat on the bed."Why didn't you pick up your phone when
I called?",he got angry."What is wrong with you?",you got off the
bed and get out of the room and walk downstairs.He grab and hold
your hand tight."Why did you change,Sharon?You've changed",he
said."Changed?You barely knew me.You're hurting me,Husband",you
said the last word with pressure.
He let go of your hand.You walk to the kitchen and drink some
water."I want to sleep",you said and walk upstairs but to your
room.You thought that sleeping separately will help.
Larry sighed.He know he shouldn't get mad but he was too tired to
think straight.He ran his fingers in his hair.



                        Chapter 35


You open your eyes.You quickly walk downstairs to check if Larry
is still around.When you are sure that Larry  is already to
work,you walk back upstairs and walk in your room.You take your
bag from the wardrobe and take out the box of pregnancy
tester.You brought it in the bathroom with you.
After you wash up,you stand in front of the mirror."Should I do
this?",you ask yourself."Just do it",you answer yourself back.You
sit on the toilet bowl and pee on the indicator.
Finish with it,you waited for a few minutes.Then,you heard your
phone rang.You pick it up."Hello?".you said."Baby,I'll be home
late today.I have something to do.Will you be okay?",he
ask."Okay.As long as you're not cheating on me",you said.He
laughed and kill the line.
You look back on the pregnancy tester.It showed two line.(Sorry I
don't know it suppose to be one line or two..hehe..XD)..You don't
know what it mean,so you refer back to the box.It's written that
if two lines meaning you're pregnant.
Your eyes widened.The box fell from your hand.You screamed loudly
and cover your mouth.You throw the box of pregnancy tester in the
trash bucket in the toilet.
You have the urge to throw up.You keep throwing up in the toilet
a few times."What should I do?",you hug your knees.You are really
worried.You're still young and pregnant.It's going to be hard.
You were hungry so you walk downstairs and fix some breakfast.You
made a simple sandwich.You carry your plate to the tv room.
You spend 6 hours in the tv room since you're so tired.Then,your
doorbell rang.You wonder who was it.

Chapter 36


You  walk to the door and open it.Your eyes widened seeing the
person who stand in front of you."Maddi,what are you doing
here?",you ask."Don't you want to invite me in?",she
asked."Uh..oh...hurm...come in",you said stutterly.She enter your
house and looked around.
"Wow.what a big house.So,where's him?",she ask you."Him?",you ask
her again."Your husband.Arrange marriage,right?",she said."I came
here to give you your homework.You've been off school for a long
time and Mrs Shim told me to give you this",she explain as she
hand you a book."She probably thought that we are still like how
we were",she added.
You look at her."Maddi,can't we be like how we used to?",you ask
her."I don't know.I don't think I can be friend with a person who
killed her own boyfriend",she said.You stunned.Maddi  was the
only person who knew about you and Richard .She knows your
relationship because she was your best friend.And you trusted
her.
"Can I use your bathroom?",she ask."Yeah,sure.But the bathroom
down here is broke down.So,you have to use the bathroom in my
room.",you said and walk upstairs.She followed you.
"Here?",she ask.You nod.She enter the bathroom.Finish her
bussiness,she stand in front of the mirror in the bathroom.She
was fixing her hair when she saw it.
The pregnancy tester on the table.She look at it.She pick it up
and look at it.
She open the door and saw you standing a few feet away."You're
done?",you ask her.She show you the pregnancy tester."What is
this?",she ask you.Your eyes widened.You totally forgot about
that thing.
"Tell me you're not pregnant,Sharon",she said with a shocked
tone.You kept quiet."I thought it was an arranged marriage,Sharon
.You made Sex with a guy you barely know?",she scream.You were
still shocked."I can't believe you're that cheap",she said and
walk out with the pregnancy tester in her hand.
"Maddi!",you call her.You reach for her before she step down the
stairs."Please don't tell anyone about this.Please",you beg
her."Let me go.Don't touch me!!",she push you.You lost your
balance.You let her go and fell down the stairs.
Your body spins and your head hits the stairs a few times.When
reached down,you were unconcious.Blood flows out from your
forehead.And slowly blood flows out from your lower parts.


Chapter 37


"Sharon .....Sharon ",Madi  call you a few times.She look at your
body and saw the blood flowing from the lower parts of your

body.Her eyes widened."I need to get out of here",she said and ran out of the house.

After running for 3 minutes,she was far enough from your house.She didn't realise that she still holding the pregnancy tester in her hand.She look around and saw a dustbin across the road.She quickly cross the road and threw the pregnancy tester.Her body was shaking.She was scared.

--------Larry At Office------

His private investigator found Sharon's friend.Larry decided to meet him.Trying to get information about that night.But suddenly,he has this weird feeling.He reach for his phone and call you.He wants to make sure that you're okay.

He called you a few times but you didn't pick up.He finally grab his coat and leave his office and drove home.

~~~~~~~~~~~

He open the door of the house."Sharon!....",he called you while looking around.He walk to the stairs and saw you lying on the floor with blood around your head and lower part.

He shake your body."Sharon....Sharon",he call you.His tears fell.He quickly lift you up bridal style and carry you to your room.He call his personal doctor to come over.

After he put down his phone,he saw the blood coming out of your lower part.He didn't even think about you miscarriage.All he thought about was he 's really worried about you.He didn't realise anything and just clean your lower part.He wipe the part with a wet towel and change your skirt.

After 10 minutes,the doctor arrived."Is she okay",Larry asked the doctor."It's weird.Is she with someone?Because the way her bruise here,you can she that she fell backward.There's no way she would fall backward alone.It's like she was pushed or something",the doctor explain.

"I'll give you prescription.You go and buy this medicine to relieve her headache later",the doctor said again.Larry thanked the doctor and send the doctor to the door.

"Backward?Pushed?",Larry said softly while thinking.


Chapter 38


You open your eyes and saw Larry  sleeping next to you.You try to sit up .But your head hurt so much.You whimper.Larry heard you and he open his eyes.

"Baby,are you okay?",he ask.You hold your head.You could feel bandage wraps around your head.He sat up and help you sit up properly."What happened?",you ask him.

"You don't remember?",he ask you back.You look at him."You fell from the stairs.",he said.You look down.You try to remember."Fell from the stairs?",you said softly.

Then,your eyes widened.You remembered.Everything.You look at Larry."Baby,how did you fell from the stairs?Was someone with

you?",he ask.You quickly shake your head."No.I-I-I was alone.",tears start collecting in your eyes.
You were worried.You were scared.You pull Larry's body and hug him with your hand wrapped around his waist and your head on his chest."How should I tell him about it?",you said while thinking about the pregnancy.At the time,you still don't know that you already miscarriaged the baby."Baby,what's wrong?",he ask you. "I'm scared",you said and tears fell from your eyes."Of what?The stairs?",he said and chuckle."No.The pregnancy",you thought to yourself.You couldn't tell him.
"Oh,and baby.I think you're having your period right now.I couldn't find the sanitary pad,so I wiped the blood.You push his body and look at him.You're eyes widened."No way",you said.",What's wrong?",he ask you.You quickly ran to the bathroom.You locked the door.
"Baby,what's wrong?",he knocked the door."Blood?So,I lost the baby?",you said softly.You smile.It's not that you don't like the baby.But,you're too young to have a baby.
"Baby,is something wrong?",he ask again with a knock."Nothing.....nothing is wrong",you said.
"It's morning already.I'll make breakfast",he said and walk to the kitchen.You look at the reflection on the mirror in the bathroom and you slightly raise your shirt.You rub your tummy."Baby,I'm sorry.I don't hate you but I'm too young to have you.",you said.
You open the door and walk to the kitchen.You saw him cooking."What do you want to eat,my queen",he ask."Dear,don't you have to go to work?",you ask him.
"No.I'm going to take care of my queen today.She's not well.",he said.You smiled.Then,a thought came across in your mind."What if he know I lost a baby?",you thought to yourself.You shake your head."He won't know",you said softly.


Chapter 39

"Baby,I need to go buy my shaving cream.",he said while putting on a white shirt.You were sitting on the bed watching tv.
"You never shave before",you said with your eyes still on the tv."I shave in the bathroom.You want me to shave in front of you?",he said and his face came close to yours.You smiled. He kiss you and walk out.
~~~~~~~~~~~
-------Reached Home-------
"Have you bought your shaving cream?",you ask him."Yeah.I gotta shave now.",he said."Take your bath too.",you said teasing him.He chuckles.
----In the bathroom----
Larry  take out his shaving cream from the plastic.He take the plastic and throw it in the trash basket in the bathroom.He threw it and walk.Then,he's stop his move.He turn back and look down in the basket.He take out the plastic again and saw a box.

It's the box for your pregnancy tester.He grab it and read the box.He frown.
He walk towards the door and open the door."Sharon ,what's this?",he ask and look at you.Your eyes widened.You quickly got off the bed and stand next to it.
"Sharon ,answer me.What is this?",his voice became louder.You don't know what to answer.You look at him,scared."Sharon ,answer me.What is this?!",he screamed.You flinched from his loud voice.You were really scared.
Your body shaking.Tears collected in your eyes."Are you pregnant?",he whimpered.You nodded."Why didn't you tell me?",he said.You kept quiet.
He turn around to the bathroom when he remembered."Blood",he whisper but you could hear him.You clutch your skirt.Your body shaking even more.He turn back to you."Don't tell me",he stop. Tears collected in his eyes."Is that why you fell from the stairs?You don't want the baby",he add.Tears fell from your eyes."No.It's not that",you try to explain."Then what Sharon?Somebody pushed you?",he said loudly.Your eyes widened. "Don't you trust me?",he ask you.Tears fell from his eyes."No.It's not like that.",you try to explain.But nothing come out from your mouth.
"Explain to me,Sharon !",he scream.Tears keep falling.He walk out of the room.Your feet felt like losing it's power.You fell on the floor.You cover your mouth with your palm and cried.


Chapter 40

Your head hurts suddenly.You hold your head with both of your hands.You whimper.Tears continually fell.Then,you led on the floor unconciously.
--------Larry-----
He sat on his chair in his office room.He bit his lips."Pushed",he said softly as he remember what the doctor told him.He then remember that there was a camera at the gate to your home.He quickly turn on his laptop and connect it with the camera.
He open the file for recording of yesterday.He waited and waited and waited.Till,he saw a girl walk in the gate.
He look closely to the screen trying to see the face of the girl.But,it's not so clear.After the girl enter your house,he fast forward the recording and saw the girl running out of your house.
"Wait,what's that?",Larry  ask softly seeing the girl holding something as she ran out of your house.Larry rewind the video and look closely.
Then,suddenly his phone rang.He picked up and a voice greet him."Sir,we've got Richard's friend.He said that he will tell you personally about what he know about that night",the private investigator said.

"Good.Arrange my meeting with him tommorow.",Larry said.He the put down his phone and look at the laptop screen again."I will find you",he said softly.

He walk to your room.He stopped in front of the door.He's getting ready to face you.He don't know what to say.

He pushes the door open."Sharon..",he call you.He look around and saw you lie down on the floor unconciously."Sharon!".he screamed.He quickly lift you up and put you on the bed.He shakes your body a few times.

But,since you're not waking up,he just try to calm himself.He then change your bandage.

"Why didn't you tell me,Sharon?Why don't you want the baby?",he said as he try to hold his tears.

## Chapter 41

-------Next Day-----

Larry  waited at a cafe,nearby your house.After a few minutes,a guy walk towards him."Mr. Brown?",he ask Larry .Larry stand up."Yes,you must be Davis",Larry ask the guy.He shake Davis's hand and sat down.

"I heard that you wanted to meet me about the fire thing.Have you met Williams Sharon?The girl that was accused to start the fire",Davis said."She's my wife now",Larry said.

"Congratulation.She's lucky.At least you're in the right mind to search for the truth.",Davis said."What do you mean?",Larry asked him.

"Since Richard died,everything change.No,actually before he died,everything changed.Since we know the relationship of Sharon and Richard",he said trying to explain.

"Maybe if you go to this address,you will understand more.",he gave Larry a piece of paper."I think I know the real person who did it.I always wanted to see the right person to be blame after Richard's death.But,I can't just frame people without any evidence.Been keeping it for two years.I can't imagine how Sharon did it.I hope you will find the evidence and put the real person behind bars.",Davis said.

"If there's nothing else,I'll go.",he bow to Larry and walk out.

------Reached His Destination-------

Larry standing outside the building.Then,he look back on the paper that Davis gave."Why would he ask me to come to a mental hospital?",he ask himself.

He then walk in the building and walk towards the front table."I'm here to see Elias",Larry said to the nurse there."What is your relationship with him?",the nurse asked Larry."Friend......old friend",Larry said.

~~~~~~~~

Larry followed the nurse to a room."He's in here",the nurse said.Larry bowed to her and walk in the room.He push the door open.

He look around the room and saw a guy sitting on a chair looking outside the window."Elias?",Larry call him.

He turn around and saw Larry.He stare at Larry."Richard,you're here?",he said to Larry.Larry blink his eyes a few times thinking whether he should said that he's Richard or not.

"Yes.It's been a long time",Larry said.Elias smiled."Come and sit here.Let's talk",Elias said and laughed.Larry awkwardly smiled.

"How was school?",Elias ask Larry."Oh...Yeah.It's normal.",Larry replied."What about Davis?He's okay too?",Elias asked.Larry nodded.

"Listen,Elias.I want to ask about Sharon",Larry said.Elias face changed."You're girlfriend?",Elias smirked.Suddenly,Elias's head shaking."She's pretty,isn't she?",Elias laughed loudly.Like a crazy person.Then,he looks at Larry

He grab Larry's collar.His eyes widened."She suppose to be mine,Richard!Mine!She suppose to choose me.Not You!!",he punched Larry in the face.

Then,he start to throw things."SHE'S MINE!!....SHE'S MINE!!",Elias throw things towards Larry.But fortunately,he could get away.

Nurses and doctors ran into the room.Nurses hold on Elias while the doctor inject him with a tranquiliser.

Larry was shocked.He quickly walk out of the room.After he walk out of the building,he sat down on a nearby bench.He wipe the blood on the corner of his lips.He sigh."What should I get from being here?A punch?What is that Davis want to show me?",Larry sighed.

He then saw a familiar girl walking in front of him towards the building.His eyes followed the girl till she's out of sight.

He try to remember where he saw the girl."Isn't that the girl who was in the recording of the camera?",Larry thought to himself.

Larry re-enter the building and try to follow the girl.He followed the girl till he saw the girl enter a room."Isn't that Elias's room just now?",Larry thought to himself.

Larry walk out again.He decided to go back home.He has a lot to think now.

-------Reached Home------

"Dear,where have you been.You're not here when I woke up",you ask him.But,he didn't answer.He just walk pass you.You move your sight to the floor."He still angry with me",you thought to yourself.

He walk straight to his office room and open again the recording of the camera.He play the video and saw again the girl."That girl is really look the same.Could it be her?",Larry ask himself.

--------At Night-----

He sat across you.He keep munching his food.He didn't say a word to you today."Dear.Are you still angry with me?",you open your mouth.He try to ignore you.

"Next time when I pregnant,I will tell.....",...BAM!!.

You flinched.You stop talking.He hit the table with his hand.A loud sound came.A loud screech could be hear when he stand up from his chair.

He walk upstairs,leaving you still on your chair.You try to hold
your tears.As you cleaning the plate and everything on the
table,tears fell.You take a deep breath to hold your
tears.But,still tears flow.
You wipe your tears with the back of your hand.
You carry the plates and utensils to the sink.You stand there and
cry.Softly.


Chapter 42


You slept in different room.You slept in your original room while
he slept in his room.
You open your eyes.You sat up and let your leg dangling to the
floor.You stare at the floor."How should I live today",you ask
yourself.
You wash up.Finish with your bath,you walk downstairs.You saw
Larry  having his breakfast alone.You fix your sight to the floor
and continue walking to the kitchen.You then hear his chair move.
Then,he walks out the door.
He drove to his office.He sat in his car after reached his
office.Tears collected in his eyes.He ruffles his hair with his
hand.He felt guilty for treating you like this.But,he's really
confuse right now.He don't know what to do.
He take a deep breath.He open the door of his car and walk
towards his building.
----------While You-------
You shut the door to your room.You lock it.You sat down on the
floor with your back against the door.You hug your knees.Your
body move back and forth.
Tears fell from your eyes.You sobs softly.
You cover your both ears with both of your hands.You kept hearing
baby's cries from last night.
"Stop it!!...STOP!",you scream hoping that the voice stop.But it
continued.The baby's cries was getting louder.
"Please....stop",you whimper.You shut your eyes and try to stop
the baby's cries.But you still could hear it.Your body still
moving back and forth.
You tightly cover your ears."STOPPP!!!",you scream at the top of
your lungs.
Then,you lie on the floor.Still concious,but looks like helpless
woman."I'm sorry baby...I didn't save you.I didn't protect
you",you whispered.
----------Larry---------
He called Davis and asked to meet him at the cafe again.
"What is it?",Davis ask as he pull the chair and sat down.
"I don't understand what's that Elias has to do anything with
this case.He's mental.",Larry  said.
Davis smirked."Don't you wonder why he  lost it?Why he got
crazy?",Davis asked Larry.
"Tell me",Larry said.

"Fine.".Elias said."Elias and his younger sister,Maddi lost their parents in a car crash.",Elias start to explain.
"Maddi?",Larry thought to himself.Then,he remembered about the girl that enter Elias's room at the mental hospital.
"Since they lost their parents,Sharon's father took care of them.Since Elias were 7 and Maddi was 5.So,they became really close.".
"As they grew up together,slowly,Elias fell in love with Sharon.He started to be obssesed with Sharon.Everything that Sharon touched,he gotta have it".
"Till,Sharon was a freshmen.We were friends.Richard ,Elias and me.I still remember the first time Elias introduce Sharon to us.He said that Sharon is like her own sister.But we know that Elias take her as more than that.".
"Then,after 3 months,there was a fight.A big fight.Between Richard and Elias .Punches and kicks were everywhere.That's when Elias found out that Sharon and Richard were dating.But,what Elias did that night was more scary".
"He try to rape Sharon.Sharon quickly reports it to the police and they catched Elias.Elias spend 5 months in lockup.In that 5 months,he lost it.His mind.So,that's how he got into the mental hospital",Davis said.
"So,he's not the real killer?",Larry asked.Davis smirked."No.But the hint for the killer is already in the story just now.How do you like it?"Dais said.
"Another question.Why did Richard's parents didn't put the charges on Sharon ?She didn't spend time in lockups or anything.It can't be that they let it pass,right?",Larry ask him.
"I thought you told me that you're married to Sharon.Don't you know?",Davis asked with his eyebrown raised.
His answer made Larry shocked

Chapter 43

It's been 3 weeks since Larry talked to you. You do your daily routine like normal but at night you would cry alone. You would lock your room and cry with hugging your knees.
While Larry already find out the truth. He already know that Maddi was the real killer. But, he didn't tell you because he thought that maybe both of you need some time alone. He also didn't put charges on Maddi yet. He's waiting for the right time.
----------Maddi POV--------
I was shopping with my friend when I got a call from an unknown number. "Hello?",I said as I pick up my phone.
"Having fun with your life?",the guy said."Who's this?",I ask him."Make sure you're having the time of your life now.Because you won't have it after this",the guy said and laughed.

"Truth will come out,Maddi.She's now investigating the case.And the truth will be known.Make sure you prepare yourself",the guy said.
My hand was shaking."What truth?Nobody know the truth and never will.I'll make sure of that,whoever you are",I said and put down my phone.
-----------Author POV---------
You were cleaning your room.Then,a call enter your phone making your phone ring.
You pick up the phone."Hello?",you said."Miss.Come home quickly.",you heard a lady speaking."What.What's wrong?",you asked the woman."Mr Park...he..he...Just come home quickly",she said and put down the phone.
You quickly got ready and walk out of your house.Larry was not in since he's at work.
You walk to the road and stop a taxi.You ask him to drive to your house.
Reached your house,people already gathered there.Your eyes widened."Dad....dad!!",you call for your father.
People heard your voice and they turned around.You continously call for your father.
"Dad.....Dad!",you call him as you enter the house.Then,your mom walk to you.Her eyes were red.Tears could be seen.
Suddenly,she slap you.In front of all the people in the house."HOW DARE YOU COME HERE!!YOU DON'T BELONG HERE!!GO AWAY!",she screamed like a crazy woman.A few other ladies try to stop her.
"Where's dad?I want to meet appa!",you said to her.Then,you walk upstairs quickly.You walk towards your father's room.
You saw a few men standing in his room.They turn as they hear you.
You look at your father.He laying on his bed,no movement.Not even his chest."Dad.....",you call him.Like a whisper.You walk towards his bed.Tears collected in your eyes.
"Dad.Open your eyes.....Dad....",you sobs trying to hold your tears.
You kneel next to him.You hold his hand.His hand felt so cold."Dad....I'm here....you're daughter is here.Please open your eyes.",you said softly.Tears fell from your eyes.
You put his hand on your cheek."Dad,please open your eyes.Don't do this to me.Please....",
Tears continue to fell.You move your hand to his body.You shake his body."Dad.Wake up.....wake up.....please don't leave me",you started to cry.
"Dad....wake up....don't do this to me.",you call him.Then,a pair of hand lift you up from the floor.But,you didn't care.You still calling for your father.
"Dad.....Dad!!....your daughter calling for you...please open your eyes Dad!!",you screamed as you were lifted outside the room and into your old room.

"Stop crying,Sharon.Stop",Larry said.You stop crying.He wipe your tears."Calm down.Don't cry",he said.You stop crying because you were scared of him.

He hold your hand and bring you out of the room.He walk to his father who was standing in Sharon's father room.

"I'm taking Sharon  out before she lost control.I hope you can arrange the funeral.I would come later.",Lzrry said.You heard him.

You shake your head and try to get off of his grab."No! i want to stay here with my dad.I don't want to leave......I don' want to leave...!!!",you screamed.

"Calm down,Sharon!",Larry almost screamed.You sat on the floor with tears still flowing."I don't want to leave.".you whimoer.You felt like you lost energy seeing your dead fatger in front of you.

Larry  lift you up bridal style and carry you downstairs.You hug his neck trying to calm down.

"Good!Take her away! i don't want to see her!!",your mother screamed while sobbing.

Larry  open the door to his car and put you.He then drive to your house.

He open the door to the house.You follow him from behind.But you walk so slow.It's like you don't have energy.left.You walk in.Then,you fell,sat on the floor.You start crying.

You cover your mouth with your palm.You crying alone.

Larry was sad seeing you like this.But,he had too much to think about.He still haven't forgot about the baby.Then,he has to solve your case.Now with your father's death,it's too hard for him to handle.

Tears fell from his eyes,seeing you crying like this.But,he didn't know if you like it if he calm you down.So,he just let you be.

After some time.You stopped crying.He walk out of the house,arranging the funeral for your father.

"Do you want to follow me?",he ask you.You shake your head."Nobody wants me there.I don't have anybody there",you thought to yourself.

You sat on your bed,with dried tears on your cheek.You lean on the headboard of the bed.You just stare blankly in the floor.

It's been hours.It's night already.Then,you heard a knock on the door."It's done....the...funeral....",Chen said and walk to his room.You didn't move a muscle.All you do is..

BREATH...


Chapter 44

Elias  put down his phone.He smirked."You're done,Maddi.",he said to himself and smirked.

------You-----

You were lying on the bed.Staring blankly at the ceiling.Eyebags could be seen.Your eyes getting darker.You didn't sleep since

your father died.You kept halucinating by seeing your father with you.You also still hearing baby's cries.
Your tears suddenly fell."Please stop it..I don't want to hear it anymore....Please.....stop it",you whisper.
You hold on your blanket.Trying to hold the anger inside.
You walk out of the room.You walk slowly cause you don't have energy.You walk towards Larry's room.
You open the door and saw Larry's sleeping.You walk inside.You stare at him sleeping.
Suddenly,he open his eyes.He turn and saw you standing.He quickly shot his eyes open and stand next to you.
He look at you.You stare at the floor.Then,you pull him into hug.You bury your face in his chest.You start to cry.
"Dear....I'm sorry....I'm so sorry....Don't ignore me like this,dear.I need you.I'm really sorry.Don't leave me like everyone else did...Please.....I beg you please don't leave me.Dad left me.I really need you.....",you cry and keep bury your face in his chest.
He then hug you back.Tears fell down.He kiss your temple.
"I'm sorry.I'm haven't been a good husband for you.I should have known how hurt you are.But I still ignored you.I'm sorry.",he said to you.
He then wipe your tears."Let's go to sleep.You look tired",he said and pushed you slowly to the bed.
You lie on the bed,hugging him and drifted to sleep.
"Soon,the truth will be reveal.Don't worry",he whispered.


Chapter 45


You were cooking at the kitchen while Larry  was watching tv.Then,suddenly your door bell rang.
"Dear.Who is it?",you ask Larry as you saw him walk out of the tv room.He shrug his shoulder.
He then walk towards the door and open it.He saw a guy in a suit standing outside.
"Can I help you?",he asked.
"Ah.You must be Mr Brown.I am Mr Jackson.I am Mr Williams's lawyer.I believe his daughter is your wife?",he said.
"Come in",Larry said.Mr.Jackson followed him.
He say across you while Larry  sat next to you."I am here as Mr.Williams's lawyer to read his will.You do know that the his company is now yours,right?",he said.You shake your head.
"I thought he gave it to mom.Even their house.He said that he will only give me a little property but that's all",you explain to him.
"Well,I guess he changed his mind.He change the company into your name.And the house is now yours too.He gave a little property to your mom.",he said.

"Here's the documents.Please sign here.",he put a bunch of papers in front of you.You grab the pen and signed.
"But I'd like to make some changes",you said while signing.
"Tell me what it is and I'll arrange it for you",he said.
You look at him."I want to give my mom the house.It won't give me any advantage anyway.I'll let her have it.",you said.Mr.Jackson smiled."I will arrange it",he said.
He put the papers in his briefcase."I hope you will take care of the company.Your father owned the company for 40 years.",he said before he left.
"I will",you said and smiled.
~~~~~~~~~~~~
"Sharon .Why don't you work at your father's company?",Larry said as he eating."But,I don't know how to work there.I'm still in school remember.Or was",you said and lower your head.
"I'll teach you.Next week.I'll work at your company and teach you how to do bussiness",he said.Your face glow."Really?you'll teach me?",you ask him.He nodded.
---------Next Week--------
You enter your father's office.It smell just like him.You close your eyes.It feels like he still in there.You open your eyes and smiled.
Larry sat on your father's chair.You bent on the desk."Teach me,teacher",you said sexily.He smiled.His face came close."Okay"he whispered.
~~~~~~~~~~~
"You do it like this",he explain."Here?",you said showing something on the paper.He nod.
"Okay.Next,type this on the computer.You always have to check the quantity.If there's something suspicious,you have to call the accountant",he said."How should I know it's suspicious?".you ask him."You just know",he said."How should I know",you ask him."Aishh! you just know",he said.You both were bickering cutely.
Then,suddenly the door was open.Both of you turn sight to the door.
"Wow.Look what we've got here.",Your mom said as she fold her arms to her chest."How dare you enter my company without my permission!",she screamed.
You stand up.You frowned."We need to talk",your mom said."Just talk here.He's my husband.He can listen to it if I want to",you said.She nod and sat on the couch in the office.Larry sat on the chair at the table while you sat across your mom on the couch.
"I thought you know that this company is mine.And you have no share in it.",your mom said."So,get out of here before I call the security",she add.
"I guess you don't get the memo.This company is mine.Says dad's will.He changed the name to me.So,I guess you're the one that have to leave this place before I call the security.Security!!!!!",you screamed.
"How dare you!!!!Do you know who you're talking to?I'm your mom!",she said loudly.

You get up from the couch and look at her."YOU'RE NOT MY
MOM!!YOU'RE JUST A WOMAN WHO MY DAD HAS TO MARRY SO THAT YOU
WON'T PUT ON CHARGES ON ME!!I DIDN'T KILL YOUR SON.I NEVER DID!!I
LOVED HIM.",you screamed.
Larry  looked at you.He knew about it.The other day,when he asked
Elias why the family didn't put charge on Sharon.Elias told him
that Richard's mother said that if Sharon's father marry her,then
she drop the charge.That's why Larry was shock.
"How dare you said you love him.After what you've done to
him!",your mother said.
"What about you?How could you call yourself as Richard's mother
when you rather marry my father for his money instead of saving
your son's name?",you said slowly.Tears collected in your eyes.
"Now turn around,walk out of this company right away.I've given
you your house.That's enough for you.Please leave this company
now.",you said.Your body was shaking,holding your anger.
"You don't even know how to do bussiness.I guess this company
will sink soon",she sarcasm."No,I will give this company to
Larry.He will hold this company",you said and smirked.
"Now leave",you said.Your mother turn around and leave.
You sat on the chair and wipe your tears.


Chapter 46


"Baby,I have meeting at my company now.So,I'll leave you
here.I'll.....pick you up at 8 maybe?",he said,standing at the
office's door."Okay",you replied and smiled to him.He walk
out.You continue doing your work.
-------While Maddi------
Her body shaking.She's sitting on her bed.Hugging her
knees."Nobody knows......nobody knows",she kept mumbling to
herself.
"I have to do something about this.I have to stop her",she
said.She raise her head.She stand up and walk outside.She walk
into her brother's room.She walk towards her brother's wardrobe
and opened it.
She grab the car keys.She walk outside and drive her brother's
car.She doesn't have any license but that's the last thing that
is inportant to her.
All she thinks about is to get rid of you.
She drove the car to your company.She waited outside.In her
car.It's two hours till Larry will pick you up.She doesn't know
that Chen would pick you up.But she found out that you would be
here cause the news stated.
News about your father's death was all around Korea.So,news about
you coming to company is also came out.
~~~~~~~~~~~

She was waiting outside in her car.Then,she saw a car came and parked across the road.She saw Larry walk out of the car and leaned on the door waiting for you.
"Ah!What is he doing here?",she sighed."Whatever.As long as I get to rid her is fine with me".she said to herself.
She then saw you walk out of the company.You were smiling seeing Larry  leaning on the door.
You then cross the road.Maddi turn on the light of the car and start driving."I hate you,Sharon !!",she screamed and drive fastly.
You were standing in the middle of the road when you realise a car coming towards you.You turn to look at the car.Your eyes widened.
Larry  too realised a car coming.He wanted to run towards you but his action was too slow.
A car hit you and you spinned.You lied on the road.The car didn't stop.Maddi continue driving.
Blood flows out of your head.Lary's eyes were widened.He ran towards you."Shaaaaaaaron!!!",he screamed.
He quickly reach for his phone in his pocket and call the ambulance.
He put down his phone after call for ambulance.He grab your head and hugged it.Blood were all over the place.Tears fell from his eyes."No.....no....please open your eyes",he kept repeating.
~~~~~~~~~~
You are in the operation room.Larry  was sitting on the chair,waiting for the doctor to walk out.
After 5 hours of waiting,the doctor walk out of the room.Larry walk towards him."How is she?",Larry  asked.His tears was still visible as he didn't stop crying.
"Her spinal cord was disturbed.The car must be that fast.Her backbone too was dislocated a bit.The back of her head had 100 stitches.",the doctor said.Then,he sighed."What is it?",Larry asked.
"She's now......paralysed from waist below.She cannot walk anymore,Mr Brown .I'm sorry",the doctor said as he hold Larry 's shoulder.
Larry's eyes widened.Tears fell.He knelt down on the floor."No....no....there must be something that you could do.What am I suppose to tell her?",Larry tug the doctors hand.He then burst to tears.
"My team worked hard.But there's nothing that we can do anymore.I'm so sorry",he said and walk away.
Larry  cover his face with his palm.He cried so hard.
~~~~~~~~~~~
He walk into your room.You were still unconcious.He sat next to you.He hold your hand.He hold your hand to his cheek.Tears slowly fell.
"I should have save you.I'm the one who suppose to lie there,not you.I'm the one who should have 100 stitches on the back of my head.",he said and cried.
"I'm so sorry,Sharon ....I'm so sorry",he said...

## Chapter 47

You open your eyes.Your sight were blurry.You blink a few
times.Your were still weak.Your head were so hurtful.You try to
sit up but you couldn't move.
You felt your hand was holding something.You tilt your head to
your left and saw Larry sleeping with his head on your bed.You
look at him.
He then move his head and rub his eyes.He lift his head from your
bed and look at you."Oh...you're awake.How your feeling?",he ask.
"My head hurt.",you whimper.He look around,trying to look for
nurse."I'll look for nurse okay?",he said and stand up from his
chair.You hold his hand."Don't leave me.",you said and look at
him in the eyes.He sat down again on his chair.
"Dear ... I can't feel my leg",you said as you try to sit.His
eyes widened.That's what he was scared of.He don't know how to
say it to you.
"Dear .....I can't feel my leg",you said again.Slowly,tears fell
from his eyes.You look at him.
"What's wrong,dear?" you ask him.He look at you with tears keep
falling.
"I'm sorry.I should have save you from that car.But I didn't.I'm
so sorry",he said and hugged you."What do you mean,dear?How could
you say that?If something happen to you,then what about me?",you
said.
"You cannot......walk anymore,baby",he said.Your eyes
widened.Tears start collected.
"What did you just say?",you whisper.He keep sobbing."Tell me
again",you add.
He let you go."How could you ask me to repeat it?It hurts for me
to say it.",he said while sobbing.
"No....It's just numb.I'll feel my leg again later.Don't
worry",you said trying to calm Larry."Don't do that.You'll hurt
yourself later,baby",he said and wipe his tears.
You look at his outfit.It's covered with blood."Is that
mine?",you ask him.He look at it and slowly nod.
You slowly crying."I can't walk anymore......can't walk
anymore....",you mumble.
~~~~~~~~~~~
"What have I done?",Maddi ask herself."She deserves it",she
answer herself."But you did to much.You killed her boyfriend.Now
you hit her",she ask herself again."But she hurt me",she answer
herself again.She lost her mind.
She's shaking.She was too scared."What should I do?",she ask
herself.She bit her nails.Tears collected in her eyes.

## Chapter 48

Maddi's doorbell rang.She opened the door.Her eyes widened seeing two male policemen standing in front of her."Are you Miss Maddi?",one of the policemen asked."Yes,..m-may I help you?",she try to stay calm.

"We're here with warrant to hold you in lock up.Please give your cooperation to ease the procedure",the policemen said again."I'm sorry,but on what charge do I has to be hold?",she asked.

The policemen took out a piece of paper.He start to read."Charge on murdering a high school student two years ago.",he said."Ah,so she didn't know that I'm the one who hit her".Maddi  thought to herself.

"Please follow us to the car",the policemen said.Maddi nodded and followed them.

-------In the interogation room------

Maddi sitting on the chair and lean her elbow on the desk.Her hands were cuffed.She's wearing a white outfit.

Then,the door was open.She look at the door and saw a woman on her wheelchair.Maddi's eyes were widened.She didn't know you were paralysed.

Larry push you across Maddi.Now,Maddi is right in front of you.Larry then leave you both in the room.

"It's been a long time.Wait,no..Since you lost your baby,right?",she said and smirked."Why did you do that,Maddi?",you ask her.Your face was frowned.

"Did what?",she ask innocently."Why did you kill Richard?Why!",you almost scream."You don't know?....you seriously don't know?",her eyebrows were raised.Then,she chuckles.

"Because of you and him,my brother lost his mind.You think I would let you go that easy?",she smirked."It's not my fault that I don't accept your brother",you said with a tough voice.

"Actually,because of you, Richard died.If you accept my brother,none of this would happen",Maddi said.

"Do you know how hurtful it was seeing him trapped in that fire?Do you know how painful it was hearing him screaming my name,calling me to help him?Do you know how it kills me seeing him trying to reach me with his hand but I didn't do anything?",you said,you bit your lips trying to hold the tears.

"Then,do you know how painful my heart is when seeing my BEST FRIEND is a girlfriend to the guy that I LIKED?",Maddi screamed.Your eyes widened.

"What do you mean?",you softly said."I liked him,Sharon.I had a huge crush on him.But you're too busy lovey-doveying with him to realise that I like him too.And then,my brother went crazy.You act like nothing happen.So,I decided to take my own action".she then chuckles.

"Then,why didn't you do anything to me?Why only Richard?",you asked her.

She laughed.Then,she whispers to you."Don't you see?Who do you think that make you sit on the wheelchair now?",she said and laughed.

Your eyes widened."How could you,Maddi!How could you!!",you
started screaming histerically.Larr then open the door and pull
your wheelchair out of the room.Maddi just look at you and
smirked.
Larry  calm you down."Stop it,Sharon..shhh....calm down...calm
down",he hugged you and rub your back up and down.Tears fell from
your eyes.
"Because of her,dear....it's all because of her.....Because of
her I can't walk anymore.Because of her I cannot pregnant
anymore",you said while hitting softly on Larry 's chest.
You guys found out that you could only be pregnant once.And you
had your chance before.Now,you cannot be pregnant again.You were
really devastated.
Larry  calmed you down.You now sleeping in the car."Call me when
the court decided on her punishment.Also,add her charges on hit
and run,and also causes my wife to miscarriage.My wife wants to
charge on the murdering,but now Maddi's too much.I want to make
sure she get her punishments right",Larry said.
He then drove home.
He carry you bridal style to the bedroom.You stare at the
ceiling.Larry  lay next to you.
"Dear.Am I that bad?",suddenly you ask Larry ."No.You're a good
person",Larry said."Then,why do God put me in this
situation?",you start to cry.Tears fell.Larry  wipe your tears
with his thumb.
"The reason that God wants to give you hardship is so that you
could have a better life later.Save the best for the last",he
said.You look at him with your teary eyes.
"Don't worry,Mrs Brown .I will make you happy",he said and kissed
your forehead.


                          Chapter 49


After 3 weeks of investigation,Maddi was put on trial.
You saw Larry  getting ready.He's wearing formal
suits."Dear,where are you going?",you ask him as he fixing his
tie.
"I'm going to the court.Today is Maddi's trial",he said."I want
to follow",you said to him."No.You just stay here,okay?I'll be
home as soon as the trial ends",he turn to you.
"I want to.I want to see her",you said.Larry  sighed."Fine.",he
said and change your outfit too.He then carry your wheelchair to
the chair,then carry you.
~~~~~~~~~~~
---------In The Court--------
You sat next to Larry,on your wheelchair.Your hand was
shaking.You were nervous.Larry  saw your hand.He then hold your
hand tight and came close to you."Don't worry.It'll end soon",he
said.You nodded.

Then,there she is.Walking with two policemen next to her.She lower her head.Her hands were cuffed.

"Miss Maddi,would you tell us the truth?About what really happen in the accident?",the lawyer said.

She lower her head.Then,she slowly raise it and look at the people.

"Earlier that day,during recess,when me and Sharon  was eating,her phone suddenly rang.She picked it up and walk outside to answer the call.I know who called her.It was Richard I was jealous of them.At night class,when she was meeting a teacher,she left her phone on her table.So,I kind of.....took the chance.I texted Richard using Sharon's phone.Tell him to meet at the janitor's store behind school.

Right after that,I waited for him to come to the store.When he reached the store,I grab a stick from the store and hit his head.When he was unconcious,I push him in the store and start the fire with a lighter that the janitor used to burn the garbages.Then,I lock the door and left him.",Maddi explain.

Only you the one who know what happen to Richard later.

You lower your head and close your eyes.The flashback came to you.Richard screaming.Calling your name.But you just stood there doing nothing.It all coming back to you.

You sobs loudly.You could not hold it any longer.The whole court hear you crying.Maddi turn to you.

Larry stand up."I'm sorry.I'll get my wife out.",he said and try to push your wheelchair.

"No!",you almost screamed.Larry try to calm you down.

"He was screaming,Maddi",you said with tears on your cheek.You look at Maddi.

"He was screaming,asking for help",you said.Larry sat back on his seat.

"He was asking for help from me.But I just stood there doing nothing.I should have save him that day",you said.

Larry calmed you down.

~~~~~~~~~~

"With this,the court announce that Miss Maddi will be in jail for 5 years and community service for 2 years",the judge said.(Sorry,I don't know how the judge say it).

~~~~~~~~~~~

"Are you okay?",Larry ask you.You nod."Sorry.Just now the flashback came and I couldn't control myself.",you explain.

"It's okay.Now,she's having her punishments.You could calm down now",he said.You smiled.



Chapter 50


It's been 5 weeks since the trial.

"Dear.Can I....meet Maddi?",you ask him as you were having breakfast.

Larry was shocked."What do you mean?In jail?",he ask.You nod your head.
"Why?",he ask you."Just meeting her",you said with your eyes fixed on the plate in front of you."Fine",he said.But you keep with your poker face.
~~~~~~~~~~
You were sitting in front of the glass.Waiting for the guard to bring Maddi.Larry was sitting on the bench a few feet away.You are sitting on the wheelchair.
Then,Maddi walk in and sat in front of you with only glass as your barrier.
"How are you doing?",you ask."Are you kidding me?How do you think when living in a prison?",Maddi scoffed.
You keep quiet.You look at a package that you brought.You show it to Maddi.
"Here,I brought you this.Do you remember?Noodles that we always eat after school.The store that was right at the corner.",you smile remembering the memories.I found out that in Korea,if you went to jail,you cannot get any job at all.So,I made some preparation for you.After 5 years,come to my house.I'll let you work at my company.I still don't know as what but,I'll give you job.You don't have to worry.",you said.
She look away,trying to hide her tears.But then,tears fell on her cheek.
"Why are you doing this to me?Why are you being nice?After what I've done to you.I killed your boyfriend.I caused you to paralayse and lost your child.Why don't you hate me?".she said.
"I hated you.But I don't see what's the point of hating you for a long time.It doesn't bring any good to you or to me.I know,you were blind with hatred and vengeance.But,it all passed.Start a new life.",you said to her.She look at you.She didn't stop crying.
You then took out something from your purse."Here,I want you to have it",you give something to her.
"Isn't this?",she ask you.You nod."Our friendship bracelet.I kept it all along.I cannot throw it away",you said."Why?",she ask."Cause you're my best friend.You're the only friend that I have.",you said.
She wipe her tears with the back of her hand."I'm sorry,Sharon .I reall am.",she said.You smile.
You look behind and nod to Larry.Larry  then stand up and push your wheelchair out of the room.
~~~~~~~~
"I'm really proud of you,baby",Larry said as he hugging you."Of course",you replied and smiled.
"Now,what will happen to us?",he ask you.
"We'll start a new life.Just you and me.Happily ever after",you said.He kiss your forehead and continue hugging you.